SELINA LAKE

Botanical STYLE

Photography by Rachel Whiting

LONDON • NEW YORK

I would like to dedicate this book to the wonderful men in my life: my husband Dave, my Dad and my late Grandpa, who sadly said 'Cherribe' for the last time while I was working on this book.

Senior Designer Megan Smith
Senior Commissioning Editor Annabel Morgan
Editor Zia Mattocks
Location Research Jess Walton
Production Manager Gordana Simakovic
Art Director Leslie Harrington
Editorial Director Julia Charles
Publisher Cindy Richards

Indexer Hilary Bird

First published in 2016 by
Ryland Peters & Small
20–21 Jockey's Fields,
London WC1R 4BW
and
341 E 116th St
New York, NY 10029
www.rylandpeters.com

Text © Selina Lake 2016
Design and photographs ©
Ryland Peters & Small 2016

ISBN 978-1-84975-713-3

Printed and bound in China

10 9 8 7 6 5 4

A CIP record for this book is available from the British Library. US Library of Congress Cataloging-in-Publication Data has been applied for.

Contents

Introduction

My love of botanicals started at an early age when my parents gave me an old-fashioned wooden flower press. I was allowed to pick flowers and foliage from the garden and press them to use in craft projects. My parents are both keen gardeners and I spent a lot of my childhood playing in the garden with my sister and being taken to visit historic gardens, plant nurseries and flower shows. Now, as a successful stylist, I find the natural world still provides a rich source of inspiration, both in the course of my work and when I am decorating and styling my own home.

Botanical Style is not just about introducing plants into your home – it celebrates a whole host of patterns and designs inspired by all things botanical. The elements of this style work with a number of themes and in this book I have explored five very different botanical looks. Firstly, 'Vintage Botanicals' shows how teaming hand-drawn prints with delicate florals creates a romantic shabby-chic look. Alternatively, you could go for a 'Boho Botanicals' festival vibe, with hanging plants and 1970s-influenced floral prints. For a more contemporary, urban feel, opt for a mix of weathered metal, bare brick and functional glassware, as showcased in 'Industrial Botanicals'. 'Tropical Botanicals' draws inspiration from the exotic, with bold leafy prints mixed with retro furniture for a glamorous effect. Last but not least, 'Natural Botanicals' is pretty and clean, featuring earthy textures and fresh greenery. I still love crafting and creating, so you'll find my 'Makes' scattered throughout, as well as 'Style Tips' that will help bring soul to any interior scheme. I hope *Botanical Style* will spark your love of nature and encourage you to bring plants, foliage and flowers into your own home.

Pressed flowers (above) can be used in so many craft projects. The *'Plantes Vénéneuses'* wall chart in my office (opposite) came from vintage shop Home Barn and I found the chair, complete with its botanical-fabric-covered seat, in a charity/thrift shop. I like to fill the house with plants and flowers, so at least once a week I head out to the garden armed with my secateurs and snip some cuttings to display in my many pots, vases and bottles.

PLANTES VÉNÉNEUSES

MORELLE NOIRE

BELLADONE

STRAMOINE

DIGITALE

JUSQUIAME

COLCHIQUE

ERGOT DE SEIGLE

BOTANICAL
Inspirations

A group of houseplants on any spare surface makes a great botanical display. There's no such thing as too many plants, and choosing varieties with different leaf sizes and shapes gives an arrangement greater interest and impact. From left to right on this marble table are a cycad (*Cycas revoluta*), Arabian jasmine (*Jasminum sambac*), fiddle-leaf fig (*Ficus lyrata*) and fern arum (*Zamioculcas zamiifolia*).

IN THE
Botanical style

Botanical Style covers a range of different style themes, from vintage to industrial, and the common thread is formed by the botanical elements that are featured throughout. Nature offers such a rich and varied source of inspiration that the decorating possibilities are endless and the simplest of interior-design choices can lead to a botanical look. Artists, designers and makers have always enriched our lives by taking ideas for shape and form, pattern and scent directly from the vast selection of plants, trees and flowers that grow all around us, and throughout time our homes and clothing have been decorated and styled with plants and flowers. Houseplants are a great place to start when creating a botanical look at home. Plants not only enhance a space but they can also have sentimental value. Perhaps a friend bought you a plant as a house-warming present and you've watched it grow over the years, or a plant may have dwelled with you in a few of

Vintage botanical books are so pretty, they should be out on display. I love the illustrations and often use open books to decorate shelves. Introducing simple botanical touches, such as a few sprigs of waxflower (*Chamelaucium*) and eucalyptus from the garden arranged in a glass bottle, is a great way to start decorating in this style.

A large wall hanging (left), *Paeonia suffruticosa* by William Clark, produced by Surface View, covers a large portion of one wall and certainly gives this dining room some floral impact. The table is laid with a vintage white lace tablecloth with a piece of floral fabric on top. A collection of vintage plates and glasses gives the space a romantic look and the black candles are a surprising and dramatic colour choice. In a few vases, pink and lime-green hydrangeas, pink and white roses, pink snowberries (*Symphoricarpos*) and white waxflowers have been brought together to make pretty posies. The blue flaking paint on the rustic wooden table (opposite) and the purple in the botanical design of the peeling wallpaper behind it are echoed by the cool, fresh tones of the mophead hydrangeas (*Hydrangea macrophylla*) and horse mint (*Mentha longifolia*), displayed in an array of simple glass vessels on its surface.

your homes, moving with you and getting taller each time. My nanna, Doreen Howard-Baylis, was always propagating plants and taking cuttings for my mother from plants like her purple passion plant (*Gynura aurantiaca*). The plants you grow yourself from seed are even more special. I love waiting for the first shoots to appear and looking after seedlings until they are established. I grow sweet peas (*Lathyrus odoratus*) each year so that I can use them indoors in vases to add scent and a pretty burst of colour. Using fresh flowers for decoration is a prerequisite of any botanical style. I like to gather a mix of flowers to make small posies, which I present in a few small vases rather than one big one. Roses, hydrangeas and even flowering mint make a striking display.

DRAWING FROM *Nature*

The natural world provides us with so much of what we need – most vitally our oxygen and food, but also our visual inspiration. Naturally occurring colour combinations found in landscapes, flora and fauna are often the most pleasing matches, and patterns formed by plants and flowers have been reproduced onto all sorts of things for hundreds of years. *Botanical Style* is inspired by the nature that surrounds us and the history we share with it. Whenever you are need of fresh ideas or a creative spark, head outside, take a walk and discover new plants. In the UK, I love visiting the Royal Horticultural Society gardens and flower shows for styling ideas for my own garden and home. Any gardens that are open to the public, flower shows, parks and forests can all be sources of inspiration, so plan a trip, pack a picnic and take a sketchbook or camera to capture some of the sights you see.

I love decorating with nature, whether I'm using wallpaper with a leafy design, fabric with a floral print or adding pot plants to a table, such as the Chinese money plant (*Pilea peperomioides*) opposite. *Botanical Style* celebrates the unique and is influenced by what is growing in the wild. If you can, pick branches of plums or sweet kumquats (*Fortunella crassifolia*), as shown here, and stand them in an oversized glass vase for a striking display. Blur the inside with the outside by using an abundance of plants in pots. Flowering herbs, such as Russian sage, thyme, mint and catmint (*Nepeta × faassenii*, above right), add a delicate summery fragrance as well as a flash of colour.

The traditional greenhouse

A greenhouse, also called a hothouse or glasshouse, is a structure with a frame built of either metal or wood and glazed with glass panels. It's where gardeners grow flowers, fruits and vegetables that need special light and heat conditions in order to flourish. Greenhouses date from the thirteenth century when they were first built to house exotic plants that explorers brought back from the tropics, although the idea of growing plants in environmentally controlled areas has existed since Roman times. In recent years, as space has increased in value, greenhouses have become multifunctional, with half the space being used for plants and half as an extra room, with comfy seating areas and tables. I love this homemade hanging shelf (above), which has been fashioned from an old plank of wood tied with string at each end and suspended from the ceiling.

My 10 favourite garden plants

1. DAVID AUSTIN ROSES If you have ever smelled the amazing scents of David Austin Roses, you will understand why I grow these beautiful blooms in my garden. The flowers are exquisite and I feel happy when the first buds appear.

2. HYDRANGEAS Few gardens are without a form of hydrangea. I love the white, pink and green versions.

3. DELPHINIUMS The tall spires of blue or white delphiniums are a must for any cottage-style garden. Use stakes to keep them upright.

4. FOXGLOVES I'm a huge fan of these vigorous self-seeders and my favourite colours are apricot and pink.

5. SWEET PEAS I grow these from seed each year. Their sweet fragrance is divine and they make great cut flowers.

6. LAVENDER The classic, sweetly scented companion for roses.

7. LUPINS Spikes of vibrant colour, best grown from seed each year.

8. PEONIES I especially love *Paeonia* 'Athena', with its apricot petals and bright yellow stamens.

9. HOLLYHOCKS Graceful tall spires studded with delicate pastel blooms.

10. SCABIOUS These annuals flower from spring to autumn if regularly deadheaded, and bees love them.

1. DAVID AUSTIN ROSES
English roses

2. HYDRANGEA
Hydrangea

6. LAVENDER
Lavandula angustifolia

7. LUPIN
Lupinus

3. DELPHINIUM
Delphinium

4. FOXGLOVE
Digitalis purpurea

5. SWEET PEA
Lathyrus odoratus

8. PEONY
Paeonia

9. HOLLYHOCK
Alcea rosa

10. SCABIOUS
Scabiosa

A fabulous 'Flowers to go' pink neon sign in the window welcomes you into florist Fran Bailey's lovely flower shop The Fresh Flower Company in East Dulwich, London, which she runs with the help of her daughters. It is a friendly place with an abundance of glorious blooms inside and out, giving the shop some serious botanical street presence. Among the plants and flowers outside the shop (opposite) is an olive tree (*Olea europaea*), dried hops (*Humulus lupulus*), white cyclamen, eucalyptus foliage, roses, hydrangeas and heather, while inside (below and right) the colourful array includes roses, gerberas and hydrangeas.

THE
Flower shop

I always love a trip to a flower shop or market, and being a stylist means that I visit them regularly to buy fresh flowers for my photoshoots. There is always something magical about discovering a new flower shop run by an expert florist and seeing the array of blooms on display, which changes temptingly with the seasons. Living near London, where there are so many amazing florists, I am spoiled for choice, but some of my favourites are The Fresh Flower Company in East Dulwich, Scarlet & Violet in Kensal Rise and Nikki Tibbles's Wild at Heart flower shop at Liberty of London in the West End. Columbia Road Flower Market in Bethnal Green, where there is a history of trading flowers dating back to the eighteenth century, is one of London's most famous botanical attractions. Every Sunday hundreds of flower stalls appear, selling beautiful seasonal bunches and bouquets.

Styling plants & flowers

Using flowers and plants is one of the most economical and effective ways to style your home or party venue. The best vases for creating big, bold arrangements are those that are wider at the base than at the neck, which makes the flowers easier to arrange (see the *Hydrangea paniculata* 'Little Lime', above). For little posies, such as the sea lavender, Russian sage, dahlias and blackberries (left) or stems of asparagus fern (opposite), a collection of smaller vases, bottles and jars gives a uniform look. Choose plants to suit the style you want to create, such as succulents for a natural space and something exotic-looking for a tropical vibe. Large plants with giant leaves work well where space allows and trailing plants add interest to shelves.

Botanicals by season

SPRING

We welcome the first signs of spring as the bulbs planted the previous autumn burst into flower, giving an array of sunny yellow daffodils, hyacinths, tulips and giant alliums. The white magnolia and cherry blossom trees begin to bloom and for a few weeks the blossom is heavenly – I always cut a few stems to enjoy indoors.

SUMMER

I have a few David Austin Roses, all with amazing scents, and my favourite season is when it's time for them to bloom. I display them in vases with larkspur, verbena and penstemons. The hydrangeas also go a little mad and the sweet peas that I grow from seed fill the air with fragrance. Lavender is also at its best and with any luck our veggie patch is providing us with fabulous ingredients.

AUTUMN

As summer draws to an end, the dahlia flowers continue to bloom. I love the dark, deep-pink versions. I like to gather a few from the garden and arrange them in dark brown glass bottles to make an autumnal centrepiece. The leaves on the trees begin to change from bright green to a fiery mix of orange and red. Collect a few and make a leaf garland by threading them onto a length of cotton thread.

WINTER

It's berry season! As we get our homes ready for a cosy winter, there's a change in the type of botanicals we want to display. Mini pine trees are a nice Nordic-style addition, and sprigs of red berries arranged in glass vases make a festive centrepiece for the dining table. Eucalyptus looks great placed in tall vessels or made into a wreath and it brings a wintery scent to the home.

FROM BLOSSOM TO BERRIES, EACH NEW SEASON
BRINGS A WAVE OF NEW BOTANICALS TO ENJOY.

LIVING WITH
Houseplants

Walk into a home filled with houseplants and you are bound to feel instantly more relaxed. Living plants clean the air, boost the oxygen levels and enhance any room they are in by lending it a fresh, organic style. After a gradual decline in popularity since their heyday in the 1970s, when plants were the must-have home accessory, the trend for houseplants has been revived and is steadily growing in fashionable circles. We've seen leafy green patterns trailing over everything from curtains/drapes to cushions, and vintage botanical prints and school charts being sought after at auctions and antiques fairs. The houseplant's renewed popularity started with terrariums, those large glass domes in which plants can be displayed, and this lead to the introduction of succulents, air plants and even large tropical plants that only thrive indoors.

My living room shows a mix of decorating ideas inspired by my Scandinavian friends: white walls, painted floors, furniture with a mid-century-modern twist and a couple of quirky touches. I love neon signs; this 'Pink' one is by Seletti. The plants enhancing the space are a delta maidenhair fern (*Adiantum raddianum*), Swiss cheese plant (*Monstera deliciosa*), *Penstemon* 'Pennington Gem' and an umbrella plant (*Schefflera arboricola*). Leading the way upstairs (opposite) are a cordyline, two delta maidenhair ferns, a Swiss cheese plant, an umbrella plant and a kentia palm (*Howea forsteriana*).

MAKE IT GREEN

This fabulous plant shop (opposite) is part of The Fresh Flower Company in East Dulwich, London, and doubles as a workshop where floral and planting demonstrations and botanical crafting take place. The rough brick walls of the former industrial space make the perfect backdrop for all the leafy plants, succulents and cacti that are for sale. A cactus painting (right) by the English naturalist John Reeves (1774–1856) has been reproduced as a giant poster by Surface View. Here, it sits alongside a collection of cacti.

So how should we display all these wonderful plants? Back in the 1970s it was all about the hanging macramé plant holder, which is still a favourite today and perfect when you are creating a boho style or if you don't have much surface space. For a more industrial arrangement, you could mix worn timber and metallic planters, and accessorize with laboratory-style bell jars and vintage bottles. In my own home I have a collection of different white pots, some ceramic and some enamel. I also like to use baskets and a few black-painted concrete plant pots. The Fresh Flower Company in London has recently opened a second store where they host workshops and sell plants alongside outdoor living and home products. It's a creative and inspiring space to visit.

My 5 favourite houseplants

Whether you've always had a few houseplants dotted around your home or you're inspired by the crop of botanical images seen all over social media at the moment, I'm sure you have your favourites. Here are a few of mine.

1. KENTIA PALM *(Howea forsteriana)*
The beautiful kentia palm has been popular since Victorian times. It doesn't need much care – just dust the leaves now and then to keep them looking glossy and lush.

2. SWISS CHEESE PLANT *(Monstera deliciosa)* A plant with interesting heart-shaped split leaves, which, space permitting, can grow super-tall. Mine is planted in a large pot, which I've put inside a seagrass basket and positioned next to my desk.

3. MIND-YOUR-OWN-BUSINESS *(Soleirolia soleirolii)* This dense, small-leafed plant comes in various shades of green. I pop them into galvanized pots and arrange them in groups on shelves.

4. DELTA MAIDENHAIR FERN *(Adiantum raddianum)* Graceful, feathery maidenhair ferns make great houseplants. I have several in white ceramic pots dotted around our living room. These shade-loving plants can also be grown in large terrariums as they need high humidity and consistently moist soil.

5. RUBBER PLANT *(Ficus elastica)*
Another large-growing plant with tropical-looking leaves. It needs some space and a little misting every now and then when the air is dry.

FOLIAGE NOT FLOWERS

Flowers have always been an easy go-to when you want to add life to a room, and foliage, despite its lack of blooms, can have a similar effect. Layer plants with different leaf shapes and textures and of varying heights on side tables, mantelpieces or shelves. Here, hearts on a string *(Ceropegia woodii)* trails over the edge of a side table and sits alongside a jasmine that has been trained into an oval shape. Tall berry stems emerge from a vintage lab bottle and hover over a shaggy mistletoe cactus *(Rhipsalis cassutha)*.

A mix of similar-sized pot plants – philodendrons, a coleus and pelargoniums – decorate the windowsill and tabletop in this simply furnished room, the colours of both the foliage and pots complementing the painted wooden furniture.

A beautiful and inspiring creative space, decorated with potted plants (a begonia and ginkgo biloba), stems of fern and cow parsley (*Anthriscus sylvestris*) in glass bottles, insect and botanical prints, and even a watering can.

Vintage
BOTANICALS

Pretty vintage style goes hand in hand with fresh wild and home-grown florals: think cottage garden meets wild-flower meadow. Inspired by old country gardens where fragrant flowers are in full bloom, romantic Vintage Botanicals are perfect for anyone who loves the vintage or retro look. Colours are soft, delicate, fresh and retro-pastel, and accessories are covered in ditzy florals and blowsy prints. As well as searching for suitable items for your home at antiques fairs, look for independent designers of furniture, textiles and artwork made from reclaimed vintage pieces.

SELF-HEALS, HOREHOU

Flower × 2

Fruit × 6

ED BELL

LAMB'S-TONGUE PLANTAIN

SEA L

BRAMBLE.

Floret × 4

Fruit × 5

CROSS-LEAVED
HEATH

Vertical section
of Flower × 4

HAREBELL

THRIFT

PLATE XLII.—1. Erigeron multiradiatus (*Many-rayed F*)
magnifica (*Oriental Bellflower*). p. 96. 3. Campanula
flower). p. 91. 4. Iris Kæmpferi (*Japanese Iris*). p. 94.
Sea Lavender). p. 99. 6. Galega officinalis, var. Hartlandii (*roc*)

251

Vintage
PATTERN + PRINT

Homes decorated in the Vintage Botanicals style are bursting with delicate floral designs and romantic blowsy blooms, from fine silks printed with vibrant colours and prettily patterned cottons and linens to hand-painted vintage bone china. Timeworn botanical books filled with beautiful illustrations are a rich source of inspiration, and the prints can be carefully torn out and used to decorate walls. I like to hang prints simply using wooden trouser/pants hangers or just tack them up with coloured washi tape for an informal look. Pressed flowers are great for making your own patterns and artwork, and they also act as uplifting reminders of the sunny summer days on which they were gathered. Pick some flowers from your garden or pluck one or two common wild flowers while you are out on a day trip and press them, then frame them and label them with the date they were picked. Group several together with toning colours to create a display with maximum impact.

VINTAGE DECORATING IDEAS

Pretty floral textiles, glorious scented roses, and flowers and berries such as sea lavender (*Limonium latifolium*), dahlias, blackberries (*Rubus fruticosus*) and coralberries (*Symphoricarpos orbiculatus*), mismatched floral china and vintage botanical books are essential ingredients for a Vintage Botanicals scheme. Use floral fabrics to sew your own cushions and pillows or buy a selection of handmade ones and use them to spruce up sofas, beds or garden benches. Freshly cut flowers, especially heady garden roses, will give any room a lift; pop stems into vases and dot them around your home, on a bathroom shelf, bedside table or mantelpiece. Use botanical books as inspiration, and rip out pages as artwork or colour copy them if you want to keep the book intact.

When it comes to choosing textiles for the various rooms in your home – for the window treatments, upholstery, table linen, bed linen or cushions and pillows – follow your instinct and pick floral prints that you are most drawn to. Whether blowsy and bold or ditzy and subtle, choose what suits your own style and in colour combinations that appeal to you. My top tip when decorating with floral prints is not to go overboard, unless you are really sure you will love the designs forever, or you are happy to redecorate whenever you get bored. I like to keep the background or foundation colours and tones of a space fairly neutral and then add botanical elements with cushions and pillows, artworks and vases, so that if I get tired of a certain print or piece, I can easily and affordably revamp the room.

FRESH VINTAGE

I love mixing old items found at flea markets and fairs with new pieces sourced for comfort and utility. This fresh vintage-style bedroom is light, bright and completely clad in wood. The comfy divan/box spring bed has been dressed simply with white pure cotton valance, sheets and pillowcases. The vintage element is introduced by means of the botanical textiles and it is easy to re-create the look with a selection of floral-print cushions and pillows. The bedroom's white foundation enables the mix of florals to work and keeps the space calm and sleep-enhancing. I often use old tablecloths as bedspreads and this lightweight throw is actually a 1970s example. Instead of bedside tables/nightstands are old wooden chairs, which are charmingly spattered with paint from previous decorating projects.

The simple shaded wall lights from IKEA, on either side of the bed, diffuse the light and help to keep the room cosy in the evening (opposite). The final touch is the pair of large glass jars of garden flowers. If you are a keen gardener and have the space, creating a patch in your garden to cultivate cut flowers is a lovely idea. I grow dahlias, foxgloves and sweet peas to use indoors during the summer.

VINTAGE DINING IDEAS

Keep the dining table simple and use little posies of freshly picked flowers and, of course, vintage china if you have a collection. I buy my pieces of old china from charity/thrift shops and vintage fairs. The floral ceramic-handled cutlery/flatware by Katie Alice works well with the vintage plates (left). Introduce botanical prints by hanging greetings cards, postcards and book pages on a display line using pegs (opposite). Hammer two nails into the wall at the desired distance from one another and at the same height, and then attach a length of thin ribbon, wire or string to each nail to create the line. I used wooden clothes pegs/clothespins, but you could look for smaller decorative pegs in craft shops.

Style Tip

For the perfect Vintage Botanical display on a dresser/hutch or shelf, stack floral vintage cups, fill a few with water and arrange freshly picked flowers from the garden (right and opposite). Here, I chose harebells, spider chrysanthemums and scabious. This idea would make a lovely table centrepiece for a vintage-inspired dinner party or wedding. You can even use teacups as mini planters. Pick out a couple that you are happy not to drink from again and put a few pebbles in the bottom for drainage. Plant small plants that don't need much space for their roots, such as pansies, in a little potting soil and water as required.

GOTT SÄLLSKAP GÖR VÄGEN KORT

I SIN FÄGRING
SOMMARN STÅR
LJUVT I SKOGEN
TRASTEN SLÅR

Morgonst
har guld i

Tag väl vara på Ditt liv
Nu är det Din stund på jorden

SMÅ SMULOR
ÄR
OCKSÅ BRÖD

Röd lyser stugan bak hängbjärkars skugga

Kä lok till min hembygds ro

ska alltid i mitt hjärta bo

VAR ÄN I
VÄRLDEN
VI BYGGA
OCH BO

HUR ÄN STORMEN VINER
BAKOM MOLNEN SOLEN SKINER

Style Tip

Wallpapering the risers is a wonderful way to bring pattern to a plain staircase. Rip off any carpet and remove tacks or nails, then sand the stairs and paint them with floor paint (I used Farrow & Ball Wood Floor Primer and Undercoat, followed by 'All White' Floor Paint). Gather up a collection of wallpaper offcuts, or rolls of the same print for a uniform look. Measure the top riser and cut out your desired paper to size. Attach it using PVA glue or wallpaper paste.

VINTAGE STYLE OUTSIDE

The extra space our deck gives us is invaluable. It is my favourite place to sit in our garden and so buying this outdoor corner sofa to furnish it was a worthy investment. Our house was built in the Victorian period and when we inherited it the garden was overgrown and uncared for, so my husband and I have spent the past couple of years restoring it. The cottage-garden style of planting includes lots of David Austin Roses, as well as foxgloves, hollyhocks, hydrangeas, penstemons and lavender. I'm addicted to buying plants and often display them on the deck in pots before they go in the ground. Here, I have dressed the sofa with a collection of vintage botanical-print cushions, which I've either made from vintage fabrics or bought from independent makers.

THE PERFECT DECORATION FOR A SUMMER PARTY IN MY COTTAGE GARDEN, THIS LOVELY PAPER BUNTING FROM PEONY AND THISTLE IS HANDMADE FROM ORIGINAL BOTANICAL PRINTS.

How fabulous is this original 1950s kitchen found in an old Swedish farmhouse? There may not be an integrated dishwasher or microwave, but forfeit these and embrace the retro – I love it. The angled wall cupboard with its sliding doors, running horizontally below the conventional run of wall units, is a great design, as the sloping front means it doesn't encroach on the workspace below. The cupboard doors still have the original green paint from the 1950s, which, along with the other green accessories and the design on the wall tiles, feels quite botanical. Many of the brightly coloured accessories shown here, such as the melamine cups and the blue and green glass lidded pots, are from Rice.dk, a great company that sells kitsch accessories for every room, many with floral designs.

VINTAGE RETRO

Introducing original pieces from the 1950s, 1960s and even the 1970s is a great way to create a Vintage Retro feel, but keep it pretty with fresh colours and floral accessories. Source vintage kitchen cabinets and units via internet auctions or commission a cabinet maker to craft something similar especially for you. If an entire retro kitchen is too much of a design statement, you could introduce retro-style elements into a modern kitchen, such as a wall-hung display cabinet or pastel-coloured kitchen appliances by Smeg or KitchenAid. Items decorated with botanical prints, including china, storage tins and serving trays, can be arranged on shelves and surfaces to create attractive displays.

Make A PRINTED TEA TOWEL

A cute addition to any kitchen is a hand-printed tea towel/dishtowel. To make one, you will need some white fabric, either 100 per cent cotton or linen, or a mixture of the two fibres, as these will absorb moisture best, scissors, a sewing machine and white cotton thread, botanical fabric transfers (mine were from eBay) and an iron. Cut the fabric to 62 x 42cm/24½ x 16½in and sew a double-folded 5mm/¼in hem along each edge. Cut out the transfers and arrange them into your desired design. Peel the backing off the first transfer and position it, face up, on the fabric. Cover it with another cloth to protect it and iron flat. Continue until the entire tea towel is covered with a botanical patchwork.

RETRO DINING

This table (opposite) is positioned to allow anyone facing the window to soak up the glorious garden view. Two pendant lights with cut-glass shades hang in symmetry above it, while pots of pink geraniums along the windowsill bring nature into the room. The fairly modern table is perfectly juxtaposed with a collection of retro chairs – an Ercol design highchair and a mix of old wooden chairs, two of which have been painted in a wonderful shade of Vintage Botanical green by Valspar called 'New Meadow'. The fresh feel of the space is enhanced by the simple colour scheme of whites and natural woods with pops of retro greens. Decoration is provided by the children's paintings, botanical prints and invitations pinned onto the vertical display line.

GREEN-PAINTED FURNITURE CREATES
A BOTANICAL FEEL. MY FAVOURITE
VALSPAR GREENS ARE 'LUSH MEADOW',
'SPRING LAWN' AND 'NEW MEADOW'.

Style Tip

Displaying your collections is an ideal way to bring personality into a space. Floral-motif tiles, plates or postcards can be grouped together to create a wall-art arrangement (above). Most DIY or hardware stores sell tile fixings and plate hooks. Lighter items, such as postcards, can be attached to the wall with washi tape or hung in frames for a more formal feature. If you don't want to search for old tiles, have a go at painting your own. Buy a pack of inexpensive white tiles from a local tile stockist and head to a craft shop for glass paints and fine brushes, and then paint your freehand designs directly onto the tiles.

URBAN LIVE/WORK

This modern London apartment has been expertly styled with a vintage feel by Katy Orme, blogger and owner of Apartment Apothecary. Katy has created a perfect balance by marrying her very modern space with her love of all things vintage. The first thing she did was rip up the carpet, which she inherited with the apartment, and paint the MDF boards that she found underneath with a light grey floor paint, after priming them with MDF primer. In the comfortable, light-filled living room, a striking, vibrantly coloured vintage kilim rug creates a focal point around which the furniture has been positioned. An old trunk makes an excellent coffee table, providing the ideal place to position glass vases of fresh flowers.

Painting one side of a door with blackboard paint is such a good idea, as it provides a great place to scribble favourite quotes and shopping lists. An array of blooming sunflowers (*Helianthus*) and gorgeous green hydrangeas placed in large jars on top of a small vintage table in the hallway creates a lovely sense of welcome.

MIX IT UP

A retro sideboard sits alongside a vintage oak table with a faded-yellow-painted base. The chairs are all Ercol originals, found at second-hand shops and online. The sideboard is a good spot for a collection of plants, as it is positioned near the large windows. On the table, garden flowers are displayed in vintage enamel jugs/pitchers.

WORKSPACE

This lovely light office/craft room/studio has a Scandinavian feel. The central double desk means that Katy and her boyfriend can work in the same space and it also serves as a sewing or crafting table. The pegboard wall panel acts as a storage space for tools and a place to pin up inspirations. The String Shelving system, designed by Swedish architect Nils Strinning in 1949, keeps books, magazines and other bits and bobs neat. The retro feel is underlined by the chairs – an original Ercol and an Eames replica.

VINTAGE DECORATING

Again, white is the base colour for this bedroom, and from ceiling to floor a soothing all-white scheme has been achieved. The traditional-style wooden bed, with its natural linen-upholstered headboard, has been dressed with plain linen sheets and pillowcases. The Vintage Botanical elements are the Abigail Borg 'Friti' cushion and a gorgeous old floral eiderdown that has been passed down from Granny. A vase of pink roses and penstemons stands at the bedside.

ROMANTIC SUMMERHOUSE

Set in a beautiful Swedish garden owned by Viktoria Johansson of Lilla Gröna, a garden design company based in Sweden, this glorious summerhouse is a wonderful place to rest, be inspired and soak up the bountiful botanical atmosphere. The little wood burner inside ensures it is well used, even during the cold winters. The custom-built wood and glass structure serves as a greenhouse for more tender plants, as well as providing a cosy horseshoe-shaped seating area around a round oak dining table covered with a linen tablecloth. Sitting inside, surrounded by all the plants, it feels as though you are outside. Create your own romantic haven in your garden by surrounding your seating area with plants in pots, complete with a grand centrepiece in a vintage garden urn or planter. Keep candles, cushions and blankets to hand for the perfect vintage evening.

VINTAGE PLANTS & FLOWERS

Decorate your summerhouse or garden room with displays of freshly cut flower posies arranged in traditional garden urns or planters instead of vases. Here, I used large hydrangea heads, fuchsias and a variety of foliage. Have you recently started growing fruits or vegetables in your garden or allotment? More and more people with a patch are being inspired by yesteryear and growing their own, including me and my husband. Last summer we grew beans, tomatoes, strawberries, fennel, rhubarb and courgettes/zucchini. Instead of tucking your plot out of sight, celebrate your growing achievements and have your produce in full view and on display. Strawberry plants make a wonderful, mouthwatering hanging basket, and vines of grapes are decorative as well as edible.

Make A SUMMER FLORAL WREATH

A wreath is a lovely decoration to make, especially if you have an abundance of flowers growing in your garden. You will need a wicker wreath as a base, which you can buy from florists, garden centres or online, and a collection of cut flowers. I used purple Russian sage (*Perovskia atriplicifolia*) and *Verbena bonariensis*, and pink sweet peas (*Lathyrus odoratus*), sea lavender (*Limonium latifolium*) and astilbe, plus some greenery. First, poke and weave the stems of your greenery into the wicker wreath until they are secure, working around the wreath to create an even base. Then do the same with the flowers. When you are happy with the arrangement, find a place to hang it up in your garden or garden room. Make a few and dot them around your garden if you are hosting a summer party.

Style Tip

Rough and rustic, and the more weathered and worn the better, wood is one of the most elementary materials to use in a garden or outdoor room. Old wooden shelves, pigeonholes and cupboards look great in garden rooms, summerhouses or sheds, as well as providing practical solutions for storage and display. Find a rough-hewn cupboard like the one opposite at a flea market or vintage fair, or commission a carpenter to make one for you from reclaimed wood. This weathered cupboard is used to display and store reference books, plants and bottle vases holding fresh cuttings. Pages from old botanical books have been stuck up with neon washi tape for extra decoration.

Boho
BOTANICALS

Free-spirited Boho Botanical rooms are relaxed, happy places with plenty of character and leafy green plants. Textiles can be summery and floaty, embroidered and silky or rich in tone and texture. Colours are deep and dark, with muddy yellows, browns and vibrant pops of colour like foxglove purples and hot pink. Furniture is from a mix of cultures and eras with inherited pieces taking centre stage. Patterns are indulgent, with full-on blooms, moody florals and classic William Morris designs. Rooms are brought to life with plants that were popular in the 1970s: think spider plants (*Chlorophytum comosum*) and pampas grass (*Cortaderia selloana*) in large ethnic vases. Layer up textures to create a fun, eclectic style with worn leather armchairs, fringing on cushions and lampshades, and bold florals.

Boho
PATTERN + PRINT

Vibrant patterns and vivid prints lie at the heart of the Boho Botanicals style, and the bold hues and rich textiles mixed with earthy plants, such as philodendrons and ferns, create a laid-back ambiance. Hugely inspired by the hippy prints that were popular in the 1970s, Boho Botanicals patterns tend to feature paisley designs and large-scale florals. Original decorative wallpapers, textiles, vases and picture frames from this era can still be found in charity/thrift shops and second-hand stores, and it is satisfying to give once-loved items a new life in your boho home. There is an eco flavour too, as retro fabrics, from clothes to soft furnishings, can easily be revamped into stylish new home accessories. For example, I inherited my nanna's home-sewn Jane Teale 'Thalia' curtains/drapes, dating from 1976, and transformed them into outdoor floor cushions to lounge on in our garden.

BOHO DECORATING IDEAS

Don't shy away from an over-the-top coloured wall. When paired with other bold colours and patterns, it will make your space look like a scene from a vibrant bazaar or souk. Hallways are a good place to experiment with strong colours. You can keep introducing plants into a boho space – too many is not possible. Hang spider plants (*Chlorophytum comosum*) in macramé plant holders, place pots of trailing ivy on high shelves and situate sun-loving fiddle-leaf fig (*Ficus lyrata*) plants near the windows. Cut flowers also play a role when you are creating a bohemian look. Bundle up some fresh flowers and hang them upside down to dry out, or gather large fresh or fake flowers with short stems to tie onto a length of string for a pretty floral garland decoration.

Introducing weathered woods and rustic elements into the mix will give your boho look an earthy vibe. Wherever possible, try to support local craftsmen and makers, and buy handmade pottery and wooden items that celebrate their raw materials. If you are drawn to an ethnic look, mix woven, patterned nomad rugs with hand-embroidered textiles, and scatter Moroccan lanterns and a couple of leather ottomans around your interior. Travelling provides the ideal opportunity to discover interesting and unique pieces to bring home. Mismatching prints and floaty curtains/drapes, sporting decorate floral designs, held back with elaborate tasselled tiebacks, complete the Boho Botanicals look.

ECLECTIC ENTERTAINING

The walls of this dining space in Strömma Farmlodge, a Swedish guest house, are hung with striking black 'Lilacs' wallpaper by BoråsTapeter and the original floorboards are painted white, which reflects the delicate white of the lilac flowers. The wooden tables and chairs are all second-hand and the mix of styles adds to the room's eclectic vibe. The dining table is decorated with a selection of grasses, stems and wild flowers, including horse mint and golden rod, arranged in glass bottles, old drinking glasses and ceramic vases. The room is lit by a collection of vintage glass chandeliers that sparkle in the daylight as well as at night. Extra lighting in the evenings comes from the candles held by the piano and lamps, with fringed mustard-coloured velvet shades, which are dotted around the room. The retro radio gives a further nod to the past.

For bold floral wallpaper in the Boho Botanicals style, check out BoråsTapeter's full range – I really like Swedish designer Hanna Werning's collection. For a quick table decoration, search second-hand shops for old cut-glass tumblers and highballs in different shapes and sizes and reuse them as mini vases for spider chrysanthemums and scabious.

Make PRESSED FLOWER TEALIGHTS

I've enjoyed pressing flesh flowers ever since my parents bought me my first flower press and let me loose in the garden with scissors, and one thing I like to use them for is to make pretty tealight holders. You will need a flower press (or heavy books), blotting paper, fresh flowers and pretty foliage, PVA glue and a glue brush, clean, smooth glass jam/jelly jars and tealight candles. Place the flowers face down between the pages of the flower press or book lined with blotting paper and leave them for 7–10 days. Glue the pressed flowers around the outside of the jars, creating a pattern as you go. Brush glue over any edges that don't stick down straight away. Once dry, put tealights inside and they are ready to use.

Style Tip

If you haven't got the space in your home for a permanent dining table or you are planning a big party, then this idea could be the perfect solution. Invest in a pair of trestle table legs (IKEA sells a variety of styles) and then either source an old wooden door from a salvage yard to use as a tabletop or, if you have the skills and tools, make your own from long lengths of reclaimed wood fixed together on the back with wooden battens. For a unique decorative idea, write a message across the tabletop using white emulsion paint and a thin paintbrush; this could be a favourite poem or quote, the date of a special birthday or wedding, or table numbers or names. Gather up a selection of chairs from around your home and dress the table with vases of flowers and candles.

BOHO BEDROOMS

The bohemian style is a great way to express your inner flower child, but before you start turning your boudoir into a hippy hideaway, decide on what aspects you are drawn to, whether earthy and eco, 1970s and nostalgic or Moroccan and ethnic. Try to use items you already own as the basis of your new style – for instance, a wooden bed frame could be painted in a vibrant shade or stained dark to look the part. Textiles come into their own here, so layer your bed with cushions, pillows, throws and blankets. These could be handmade from vintage scarves or bought from outlets such as Anthropologie. Display your favourite boho clothes on a metal rail or hang a special dress from a hook or nail with a bundle of drying flowers. Flooring can mirror the bed dressing, with overlapping suzani rugs and piles of cushions. Colourful rugs, heirloom quilts and fringed embroidered shawls can be used to adorn the walls.

This old hospital-style metal bed (opposite) doubles as an inviting daybed, dressed with layers of Indian patchwork throws and a selection of cushions. The handy Moroccan green leather ottoman is the boho way to put your feet up. The hand-crafted wooden stool is the perfect height for a beside table/nightstand, with a green Anglepoise task lamp that adds a slightly industrial feel to this cosy nook.

Make SILK SCARF CUSHION COVER

Beautiful vintage silk scarves are perfect for making cushions and pillows to adorn a boho bed or sofa. You will need a square silk scarf, co-ordinating fabric for the cushion backing (I used natural linen), matching cotton thread, fabric scissors, a sewing machine and a cushion pad/pillow form. First, measure your scarf and decide what size cushion to make, bearing in mind the size of your cushion pad and how much of the design you want to see on the front of the cushion. Cut the scarf to the same size as the pad, adding 1.5cm/⅝in onto each side for the seam allowance. Measure and cut two pieces of fabric for the backing — each piece needs to be the same width as the front panel but one-third shorter in length. Sew a hem along one width of each back piece. With right sides together, layer the two back pieces on top of the front panel with the hemmed edges overlapping in the middle to make the opening. Pin and then sew around the outside of the square. Turn the cushion cover right side out and insert the cushion pad.

SAY IT WITH FLOWERS

Some of these paintings were done by my nanna, Lilian Rose Lake, and I treasure them (above). When displaying floral artworks, don't hold back but mix oil paintings on canvas with watercolours and floral botanical prints for a rich collection. To make more of a few freshly picked flowers, arrange each stem in a different glass vessel and group them together on a sideboard or dressing table. Here (left) is a colourful mix of larkspurs, penstemons, marigolds, hydrangeas and roses.

BOHO HALLWAYS

Don't forget spaces like entrance halls, corridors and landings, where you can be more experimental in creating a boho mood. Paint doors and woodwork in unusual colours – botanical greens always make for an interesting look, and emerald and aqua both work well. Choose a bold wallpaper, such as the classic William Morris 'Golden Lily' design in indigo (opposite). Hooks can become a display area for favourite leather handbags, hats and coats, as well as posies of flowers or herbs and hanging plants. Unsightly items can be hidden from view under the stairs or in an alcove by a curtain made from a vintage tablecloth. If you have room, add a stool for putting on shoes and display tall stems, such as dried fennel (*Foeniculum vulgare*), in a French antique green glass wine flagon.

DARK FLORALS

The trend for all things dark and floral has migrated from the fashion catwalks into our homes. In this living room of a London townhouse, 'Dark Floral' wallpaper by Ellie Cashman Design makes a dramatic statement. The large-scale painterly floral, with its cascades of majestic roses, peonies and chrysanthemums set against a deep, moody background, was inspired by the still lifes of the Dutch Golden Age. There is no need for showy floral arrangements here, as the walls do all the talking, but a few limited-edition porcelain insect vases by Thomas Eyck adorning the chimneybreast wall are the perfect vessels for single rose stems. The contemporary copper table lamps give the room a modern feel, while pops of botanical green on the cushions and upholstered armchair ensure it isn't gloomy.

Fans of dark floral prints should check out Ellie Cashman Design's full range of fabrics, wallcoverings and cushions. House of Hackney is also worth exploring. Its prints adorn clothes and furnishings alike, and the Midnight Garden collection, inspired by blooming country gardens at night, will bring a romanticism to any interior.

Display is an important aspect of any Boho Botanicals look. In this bedroom (left), a wall of mainly monochrome artwork brings the scheme to life. The mix of styles is united by the tones of black, white and grey, with pops of blue and purple to tie in with the turquoise glass vase and the striking floral bed with its collection of botanical cushions. In the kitchen (opposite), the eye-catching canary-yellow shelving unit, by Danish company Montana, provides a great storage and display space for books and vases.

URBAN GLAMOUR

As well as the hippy floral vibe and the ethnic, earthy look, spaces decorated in the Boho Botanicals style can take on a more glossy, glamorous appearance. The key is to start with a chic, neutral backdrop, as in this bedroom (above) with its pale-grey walls and dark-grey woven carpet, and then introduce luxe materials and furnishings, such as plush upholstered beds, and contemporary designer fittings, for instance the Caravaggio lights by SCP that hang in this urban kitchen (opposite). The trio of matt pendant lights provide a textural contrast with the polished marble surface below, and their sage-green colour ties in with the botanical shades in the furnishings, ceramics and kalanchoe plants. The punchy fabric used for the blind/shade is 'Chanter' by Etamine from Zimmer + Rohde, and the floral rug designed by Nathalie Lété brings an eclectic feel to the room.

ON DISPLAY

The relaxed Boho Botanicals home celebrates a mix of styles. Instead of hiding away a collection of vases, make a display of them. This selection of glass and ceramic vessels, holding stems of orange roses and purple campanula, shows how jade, turquoise and blue sit in harmony with dusky pink, lilac and plum tones, complementing the bold prints on this corner sofa and silk-scarf cushions.

Industrial
BOTANICALS

Decorating to achieve an industrial look has been a growing trend over the past few years, with old office and industry furniture being sought after at flea markets and antiques sales. Think battered wooden cabinets, metal pendant light shades and items that were once used for educational purposes at schools. Old lab bottles have been reinvented as stylish vases, and science wall charts, which used to hang on classroom walls, are now super-trendy. In this chapter I slightly soften this rough-edged style by adding masses of greenery to create Industrial Botanical schemes.

Industrial
PATTERN + PRINT

The Industrial Botanicals style is not particularly renowned for incorporating loads of pattern, although introducing botanical designs into an industrial space can soften the look and add interest, especially to the walls. Vintage monochrome botanical designs will fit in perfectly with this style of interior, as well as botanical wall charts and old school posters, which are much in demand at the moment. Decorating the walls with posters and prints is an easy and fairly affordable way to update your space. Look for designs depicting plants and insects – I'm especially fond of designs that include stylized foliage and dragonflies. Original botanical charts from the 1960s and 1970s are quite expensive and can be hard to source, so check out Wallography, a British company that reprints old plant designs, and Hagedornhagen, a Danish company formed by two photographers that produces photographic prints of butterflies, beetles, leaves and flowers.

INDUSTRIAL DECORATING IDEAS

Black may seem a harsh colour to paint a wall in your home, but trust me, it's the go-to hue when creating an Industrial Botanicals style, as it will make green elements pop. The other colours synonymous with this style are emerald greens, glass browns, concrete greys and wood tones. Unless you live in an old loft or warehouse, you'll need to create the illusion of rough surfaces and materials that suggest an industrial past. The simplest way to do this is to leave some walls or surfaces unfinished. Recycling is also a key part of this trend – old pipes could be revamped into rails for hanging clothes and vintage packing crates make stylish bedside tables/ nightstands. Source original tripod lamps from antiques shops and use old metal chairs around your dining table.

Other patterns in this style rely on the textures and patina of second-hand items or the surfaces of walls, brickwork, bare plaster or rusty metal. Look for wallpaper that represents these rough surfaces and remember that dark backgrounds will make green patterns stand out best. Textiles are on the natural side, with linens and well-worn leathers coming into their own, but an amazing floral-print dress could be hung on a vintage metal locker to be admired almost as a piece of art. Furniture is a mix of wood and metal, and old metal shelves on wheels are perfect for an Industrial Botanicals display. Dried globe artichoke flowers (*Cynara cardunculus* var. *scolymus*) make lovely decorations, with their architectural shapes and blue, purple or pink centres. Hang the flowers from their stems for a few weeks to dry.

BRING THE OUTDOORS IN

This lovely space is a Swedish flower/plant shop and café called Minaidéer. It is situated in an old timber building and has walls clad with a mix of woods, as though they have been patched up over the years. Tina von Wowern, the owner, has brought the outdoors in and created a cosy haven, with comfy armchairs dotted around so that shoppers can enjoy a cup of tea while they browse.

Plants are displayed in woven baskets and there is greenery everywhere. To re-create this effortless style at home, you will need a selection of baskets that can double as planters, faux-fur rugs to soften armchairs and some botanical posters. Invest in a worn timber table and use black metal 'Model A' Tolix chairs to keep with the industrial theme. Glass bottles holding flowers or foliage will add an outdoorsy feel.

Hanging baskets, wooden crates and metal bowls all make great places to display plant life in this space. Fill a wooden box with green and brown glass bottles and add single stems of ferns for an easy Industrial Botanicals display. Shallow metal dishes make great homes for groups of succulents. Have a go at making your own hanging planters by adding lengths of string to woven baskets.

EXPERIMENT WITH DIFFERENT CONTAINERS AND WAYS TO HANG YOUR PLANTS. MACRAMÉ IS A GREAT SKILL TO MASTER, AS WELL AS KOKEDAMA.

HANGING PLANTS

A mistletoe cactus (*Rhipsalis cassutha*) and a red coral plant (*Pseudorhipsalis ramulosa*) hang together from a rope ladder in this warehouse space (above). Kokedama, a Japanese style of planting that uses moss to retain moisture instead of a pot, has become a popular way of hanging plants. Remove most of the soil from the plant until the majority of the roots are exposed (except plants that wilt easily, such as coleus and ferns, whose root balls should be left more intact). Mix peat with akadama (a soil used for bonsai trees) until the mixture is wet. Attach it to the roots to make a ball shape, then build up the shape with moss. Secure the moss with string and make a long loop for hanging.

Make A METAL HANGING BASKET

This hanging basket of herbs is made from an old metal jelly/jello mould and chain from a hardware store. You will need a suitable lightweight metal container, a metal punch, three equal lengths of chain, and pliers. Punch three holes an equal distance apart just under the brim of the container. Using the pliers, open a link at one end of the first chain and insert it through one of the holes, then squeeze it together again. Repeat with the other two holes and chains. Gather the chains and join them at a place where the container stays level, using the pliers to open and close the loops as before. Add pebbles to the base of the container for drainage, fill with soil and plant your herbs.

Make A HANGING LIGHT-BULB VASE

Recycle old filament light bulbs to make hanging botanical decorations. If you can, remove the base of the bulb using a small screwdriver, wearing protective gloves and glasses in case you break the glass, which I did on a few occasions. Then take the filament section away. Tie string around the metal part of the bulb, ready for hanging, then fill the bulb with a little water and pop in a couple of sprigs of greenery. If it proves impossible to open up your bulb to make it into a hanging vase, you could simply tie the stems of the plant cuttings to the end of the bulb with string to make a hanging decoration without the fuss.

I love these beetle and butterfly prints from Hagedornhagen, a Danish company founded by photographers Mads Hagedorn-Olsen and Anders Morell. Sprigs of fern and fennel from the garden in clear glass bottles and the bright green fan-shaped leaves of the ginkgo biloba plant pop out against the black wall behind them, while the two ornate black frames hanging on it almost fade into it. Black storage boxes make it easy to keep the desk area neat, and a couple of old books bound in green leather and tied with string add a decorative touch to the pile of garden-design books.

THE ARTIST'S STUDIO

All the artist's studios that I've ever visited seem to have a special charm, and this studio space in a seventeenth-century stone cottage in Sweden owned by artist and florist Marie Emilsson is no exception. It is a stylish, creative space where crafty bits are stored away in an industrial locker, a wooden crate is home to bundles of yarn and wool, and magazines and books are piled high. The long desk in front of the window is fashioned from a length of MDF resting on top of black metal IKEA trestles and the chair is made of wood that has been stained black. Insect prints from Hagedornhagen hang from black metal bulldog clips on the black-painted wall. A large filament light bulb lights the desk area once the sun goes down, and plants in terracotta pots – a begonia and a ginkgo biloba – bring organic forms and flashes of green into the space.

A lovely idea for an industrial wall is to display a collection of botanical prints using bulldog clips to hang them (opposite). Most of these are printed illustrations by Ingrid Jacob from *The Illustrated Book of Herbs* by Gilda Daisley (1988). I found a copy in a charity/thrift shop and tore out the pages to decorate the wall. The two rose prints are from *An Illustrated Treasury of Redouté Roses* by Frank J Anderson (1979) and the metal bulldog clips came from an office supply store. If you want the prints to hang super-straight, use a spirit level and tape measure, but I did it by eye. Decide how far apart you want the prints to hang by holding them up against the wall. Mark the position of the first nail with a pencil and hammer it in. Hang up the first print to get an idea of spacing, then mark a guide for the second nail. Continue until you are happy with the collection.

MAKE IT POP

I have already championed the idea of going dark with your wall colour, and if you weren't convinced before, perhaps this stunning image (above), taken at Minaidéer in Sweden, will make up your mind. I love how the peach and pink gladioli blooms stand out against the black backdrop. Plants look amazing against the darkest shade too. Introduce elements of black slowly, if you are unsure, such as painting a single wall or the back of a shelf unit. 'Pitch Black' Estate Emulsion by Farrow & Ball is my choice.

INDUSTRIAL DECORATING

This artist's studio is packed with canvases and frames awaiting new works of art. Art and craft supplies are stored away inside the old green metal triple locker. The stunning embroidered mint-green coat with floral lining softens this side of the room. A spattered old paint case is displayed on the windowsill next to a weeping fig (*Ficus benjamina*) and white gladioli stems in a glass bottle.

GARDEN RETREAT

How lovely is this garden room, designed by its owners artist Marie Emilsson and her partner. Essentially, it's a greenhouse, a wooden structure painted grey and panelled with glass windows sourced from a flea market. Inside, a metal daybed provides a place to relax, and around the table a mix of chairs gives the space an eclectic feel. I love the combination of wood, rattan and metal. The grey colour of the framework adds an industrial element, along with Marie's vast collection of green glass bottle vases. A fig tree (*Ficus carica*) happily grows in the corner, and at the front of the space a wooden potting bench makes a great place to store lovely gardening paraphernalia. Electrical wiring has been connected to the garden room so that the space can be enjoyed into the evening, when pretty light effects are created by the woven lampshade and a few candles makes it feel like a romantic retreat.

An old French metal folding table is positioned in front of an abundance of ferns in the garden (left). The metal and wood chairs were once painted bright turquoise and are now a mix of worn, faded paintwork and a little rust. Oversized green glass bottles make great vases for tall garden cuttings. Find garden furniture similar to this at vintage shops and markets. I have a couple of French metal folding tables that I use in the garden to display pots and stoneware.

A warehouse wall that has been distressed over time is difficult to imitate with paint effects, so look for unusual patterned wallpapers with a similar feel, such as the fabulous and realistic 'Concrete' wallpapers by Piet Boon. A large old metal trolley (opposite) is the epitome of industrial style and here it is used to display a mass of plants – including a cordyline, mind-your-own-business and a variety of ferns – and fresh foliage cuttings arranged in a selection of glass bottle vases and plant pots. A Boston fern (*Nephrolepsis exaltata*) hangs from one side of the trolley, while an old glass bottle displaying stems of *Amaranthus caudatus* 'Green Tails' sits on the floor beside it. An old door (right) makes an interesting backdrop for hanging another Boston fern and a spider plant (*Chlorophytum comosum*) using string macramé holders. The well-worn leather armchair was bought from an antiques shop specializing in vintage industrial style.

WAREHOUSE SPACE

If you don't happen to live in a converted old factory building, how do you create a convincing and stylish Industrial Botanicals home? It's all in the details, so invest in a few key pieces that have a past and were once used in the workplace – items such as an old metal locker or a pigeonhole cabinet for storage can be sourced from specialist dealers. Then look at lighting. Many mainstream retailers sell lights inspired by the types of lighting used in industry, for instance oversized filament bulbs, metal pendants and wood or metal task lamps. Once you have the basics, start to incorporate the botany, keeping it green and plentiful rather than too floral. Look out for old science-lab bottles at flea markets and collect a variety of sizes to use as vases. Introduce botanical-print textiles with dark backgrounds and vintage educational botanical wall charts and illustrations.

Make YOUR OWN CONCRETE POTS

The perfect plant pots for an industrial-style space
are concrete or metal. Have a go at making your
own from cement. You will need plastic plant pots
of different sizes, with smaller pots sitting inside
bigger pots with a border of at least 1cm/½in,
strong duct tape to tape up the holes in the base
of the pots to stop the cement from seeping out and
a small bag of concrete mix from a hardware store.
Following the instructions, combine the concrete
mix with water in a large plastic bucket. Pour a
little into the first larger pot to make a base, then
place the smaller pot inside and add the rest of the
cement. You need to work quickly, as the concrete
will start to set and it will be easier with someone
to help you. Once dry, cut away the plastic pots to
reveal the concrete planters.

Tropical
BOTANICALS

Inspired by the glamour of the Beverly Hills Hotel with its iconic banana-leaf 'Martinique' wallpaper – designed by Don Loper in 1942 and still in production (see the front cushion, above) – and its neon electric light signs, which gained popularity in the USA between 1920 and 1960, the Tropical Botanicals style is retro, fun and jungly vibrant. Bring tropical greenery into your space with statement plants such as giant palms that will evoke a glamorous retro feel. Go all exotic and play around with tropical prints, which you could wear as well as decorate with.

Tropical
PATTERN + PRINT

Lush, vibrant, brash and bold, this style of botanical print is not for use by shrinking violets. Designs are usually large-scale and energetic with swirling leaf forms, creeping foliage and exotic blooms in bright, rich colours that bring to mind tropical rainforests, palm-lined beaches and the undeniable glamour of locations such as Hawaii and Palm Springs in their heyday in the mid-twentieth century. The colours are invariably deep and saturated, with an abundance of dark leafy greens and peacock blues plus oranges, pinks, purples and turquoise thrown into the mix. As such, interiors can be brightly coloured or predominantly white to give these tropical patterns breathing space. Wood, rattan and wicker furniture complement these prints, whose organic curves and whirling forms will serve to soften the hard edges of contemporary interiors and also work well with mid-century pieces.

TROPICAL DECORATING IDEAS

Embrace this style wholeheartedly and be bold in your use of tropical prints. Select wallpaper with lush, leafy designs that will give your room an exotic feel, and furnish the space with wicker or bamboo furniture for a natural vibe or go all out with chairs upholstered in a bold, tropical-print fabric. House of Hackney offers a fabulous range of quirky homewares and fashion accessories that are perfect for fashionistas and tropical fans. I particularly love their 'Castanea' design, featuring green leaves and flamingo-pink flowers, and I used the wallpaper and matching scatter cushions in my bedroom (see page 108). Adding a collection of cactus, ferns or succulent plants, such as echeverias (above centre), to your space will also give it a tropical twist.

Tropical patterns seem to be popping up on everything from fabrics and wallpapers to kitchen accessories and lighting, with new designers being inspired by the glamour of exotic designs. Tropical-leaf wallpapers might seem too summery to adorn the walls in your home all year round, but that being said, a flash of tropical fun and lush vegetation might be all you need to boost your mood on a dark and gloomy winter's day. For tropical colours, use zesty lime green and rainforest greens with dashes of flamingo pink and natural cane. I have found several independent makers who have been inspired by tropical colours and designs, and I particularly love the Heart Vintage's upcyled vintage tropical plates and prints (see previous spread).

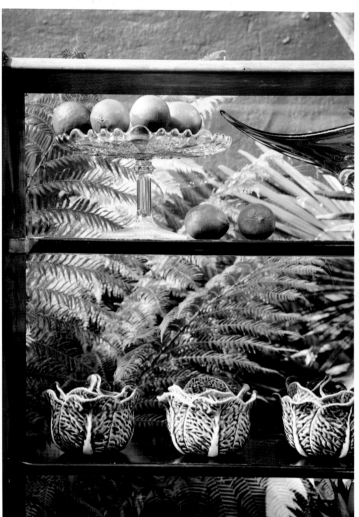

TROPICAL GLAMOUR

This glass-cube garden room is a somewhat unique find in a London property. Originally built for a television show on garden makeovers, the glass box is suspended over a large fish pond and sits inside a tropical garden designed by the Irish garden designer and television personality Diarmuid Gavin. The current owners of this fabulous oasis use it as a place to relax and drink green tea or maybe a few cocktails while soaking up the sun. The cube is furnished with a mid-century wooden sideboard and dresser/hutch, which doubles as a bar during parties in the garden. The surrounding wall has been painted the bright blue of summer skies and together with the lush planting, which includes a tree fern (*Dicksonia antarctica*) and a Chinese windmill palm (*Trachycarpus fortunei*), enhances the tropical feel.

This tropical garden was designed by an expert, but if you want to achieve a similar style of planting, the best place to start is at a specialist stockist of tropical plants, which you can find online. Visit with a rough idea of what you are trying to create and make the most of any advice. Large plants are expensive, so build up layers of ferns, hostas and palms if you are working to a tight budget.

TROPICAL OASIS

Key ingredients are a comfy chair or garden sofa in
rattan or bamboo; cushions with palm-leaf designs,
like these by Sketch Interiors, painterly florals or in
plain jade or neon-yellow velvet; and a lush mix of
topical plants, including cactuses, palms and ferns.

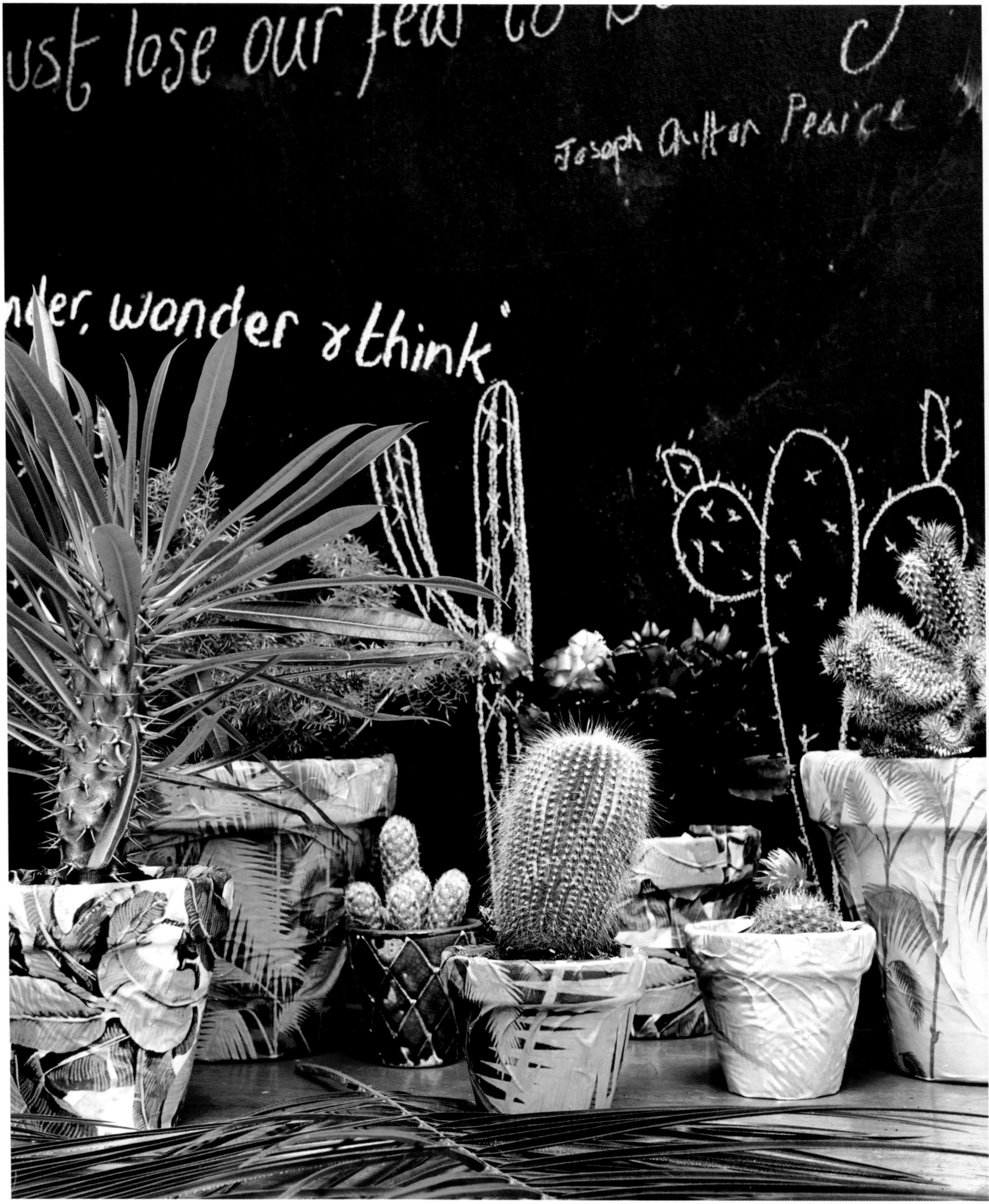
ust lose our fear
Joseph Chilton Pearce
der, wonder & think"

Terrariums, which originated in the Victorian era, act as mini greenhouses and create microclimates for certain plants that need shelter, light and heat. In recent years it has become a popular trend to use them indoors as decorative plant containers, but the glass domes can also be used outside to protect plants from harsh weather conditions and to grow hardy cactus or succulents, especially in rockeries. Plastic domes don't cut it in the style stakes, so look for vintage glass domes at antiques fairs or new ones at garden centres to display plants such as a houseleek (*Sempervivum*), shown left.

Make WALLPAPER-COVERED PLANT POTS

This idea works for all botanical styles, but a tropical look is perfect for potted cacti. You will need tropical-print wallpaper samples – I used 'Banana Leaf' by Martinique, 'Palm Jungle' by Cole & Son, 'Honolulu Palm' by Julien Macdonald and 'Tropicana' by Osborne & Little. You will also need terracotta plant pots with drainage holes, scissors, PVA glue and brush, and clear varnish and brush. Lay out your wallpaper and roughly gather it around a pot to assess the size needed, add a little excess and cut to size. Paint the back of the paper with glue and mould it around the pot. Wrap any extra paper over the rim or cut it off. When the glue is dry, paint on a thin layer of the clear varnish.

Style Tip

Create exotic patterns on your walls with a selection of fresh tropical leaves bought from your local florist. I used the frondy leaves of a pygmy date palm (*Phoenix roebelenii*) and heart-shaped Swiss cheese plant leaves. Arrange them across your wall and tape them up with neon washi tape for a fun look. The leaves will stay green for about a week. For a more permanent display, you could opt for faux leaves – Abigail Ahern sells a beautiful range of jungly faux leaves and stems, from California buds to banana leaves, which will last and last. This is a great idea for a tropical-themed party too.

ADD SOME TROPICAL BOTANICALS TO YOUR BEDROOM WITH QUIRKY CUSHIONS AND PILLOWS, TROPICAL-LEAF DECORATIONS AND A FEW POTTED PALMS.

INDOOR GARDEN

This indoor courtyard has been transformed into an exotic hideaway that looks like something straight off a set from the musical *South Pacific*. Who knew these Victorian wicker peacock chairs would come into their own again? As bamboo and wicker furniture has become highly fashionable once more, original conservatory furniture is being given new homes in our living rooms and bedrooms, and it is the perfect choice for a Tropical Botanicals space since it is made directly from plant fibres, cane, willow and raffia. Danish company Bloomingville has a great selection of similar furniture. The tiled floor is an added bonus, as it makes spillages from watering plants easier to clean up. Talking of plants, this fabulous sun parlour is brimming with palms, ferns and zebra plants, which all thrive under the direct sunlight streaming in through the glass roof. Key plants, clockwise from left to right, include a zebra plant (*Calathea zebrina*), kentia palm (*Howea forsteriana*), Chinese windmill palm (*Trachycarpus fortunei*), Boston fern (*Nephrolepis exaltata*), Philippine orchid (*Medinilla magnifica*) and a kalanchoe.

> The cushions are made from Tommy Bahama 'Swaying Palms Aloe' fabric, which is stain- and water-resistant, making it ideal for use in a garden room or outdoors. You could also make your own cushions from vintage Hawaiian shirts with bold leafy and floral hibiscus designs.

Make A GLASS JAR TERRARIUM

So, you're keen to try out the terrarium trend but not sure where to start? Cactuses are great plants to begin with, as they are fairly self-reliant and won't die if you forget to water them for a week or even a couple of months. Find a large glass jar or container and head to a garden centre where you'll discover an array of colourful, even flowering, cactus plants – I chose a Christmas cactus (*Schlumbergera*). Put a layer of small stones in the base of the container for drainage, then pour in fast-drying soil that retains some moisture and plant your cactus, wearing rubber gloves to prevent injuries from the needles.

PLANT STANDS

Other than hanging plants from the ceiling in a basket or macramé holder, or trailing them over the edge of a shelf, another great way to display plants with droopy foliage is to arrange them on a plant stand. At antiques fairs, look out for vintage metal plant stands that you could use outside or in your garden room. You could also use metal trollies or stools.

I love this emerald-green wall colour. It's the perfect shade for a Tropical Botanicals space and the distressed condition of the battered wooden panels only adds to its charm and impact. The industrial feel of the bare concrete floor and the metal table, chairs and vintage trolly are softened by the bright mix of tropical floral fabrics on the dining table and the quirky containers for the arrangements of exotic blooms and individual leaves. The vibe is fresh, uplifting and full of fun.

TABLE STYLE

Your tabletop is a great place to experiment with tropical prints, as the lively patterns and vibrant colours will energize and stimulate your guests. So gather together a selection of napkins, placemats and fabric offcuts, all patterned with tropical foliage or flowers, and layer them up to create a patchwork tablecloth. Here, I used a combination of fabrics from Zara Home, Michael Angove and Kith & Kin. Industrial items mix in well with the tropical look and this rusty green metal trolley makes a good movable bar. The leaf-green metal folding chairs from Habitat are a great addition to this dining setting and can be stored away easily when not in use. The bold, green-painted panelled wall is a fabulous backdrop and goes to show that not every surface in your home needs to be perfect; peeling paint adds interest to your party paradise.

TROPICAL TABLE STYLING IDEAS

A neat idea to give your drinking glasses a tropical twist is to wrap them with fresh banana leaves and secure them in place with narrow neon-pink ribbons. For a fun centrepiece, turn a humble pineapple into a fabulous vase. Take a big pineapple, the biggest you can find, as this will make the most dramatic statement in the centre of your table, and chop off its crown leaves with a sharp knife (please mind your fingers). It can be a little tricky to remove the flesh from inside, so take your time and feel free to nibble the sweet fruit as you go or save it to eat later. When it is hollowed out, you can either fill the pineapple with water, as long as there are no leaks – test it first before placing it on your table – or fill a glass or small vase and stand that, unseen, inside the pineapple. Now arrange a selection of tropical-looking flowers and greenery in the pineapple container. I used coral-coloured begonia flowers, yellow Billy buttons (*Craspedia globosa*), *Leucospermum* 'Tango' and proteas.

DRAW COLOUR INSPIRATION FROM THE HUES OF EXOTIC FLOWERS. BEAUTIFUL PEACHY CORAL BEGONIA FLOWERS AND RAINFOREST GREEN MAKE A PERFECT COMBINATION.

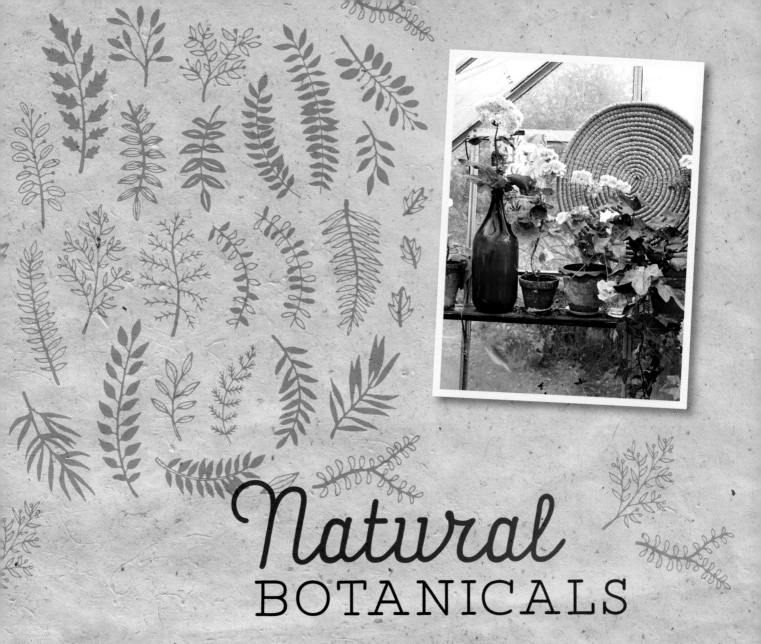

Natural
BOTANICALS

Simple and stylish, Natural Botanicals interiors feature a gentle mix of textures. Untreated woods work in harmony with white-painted furniture for a clean, calm style that gives a nod to Scandinavian interiors. Woven baskets make perfect plant holders and soft furnishings are fashioned from linen, cotton and worn leather. Plants and greenery give these neutral spaces character and interest. The colour palette is based on whites, soft greys and putty shades combined with organic greens, natural wood and touches of pure black.

PLANTS. THEIR NATURAL GROWTH AND ORNAMENTAL TREATMENT.
BY F. EDWARD HULME, F.L.S.

PLATE V

44 ROCHESTER.

45 OXFORD.

46 ROCHESTER

47 ROCHESTER

SYCAMORE.

ACER PSEUDO-PLATANUS.

48

49 CANTERBURY

LILAC

SYRINGA VULGARIS

CAPSELLA BURSA-PASTORIS.

51

52

53

54

55

ACER PSEUDO-PLATANUS   SYCAMORE.

56 CAREX VULPINA.

57 ALISMA PLANTAGO

SPIRÆA ULMARIA

58

59

60 SAMBUCUS NIGRA

LAMIUM ALBUM

62

63

SHEPHERD'S PURSE.

64

65

RADISH.

RAPHANUS SATIVUS.

ROCHE ABBEY.

MARCUS WARD & Co. LONDON & BELFAST.

S.B.F. 4   *Phegopteris Robertiana*

115

114

PLANTS

THEIR NATURAL GR

AND

Ornamental

BY

F. EDWARD HULME, F.LS.,

161b

163

163a

161a

161c

161d

161e

164

163 Hop *Humulus lupulus;* female plant with hop cones 161a Male
flowers 161b Female flowers 161c Single male flower 161d Two
female flowers with bract 161e Insect with lupulin glands

164 Beer Yeast (very highly magnified) *Saccharomyces cerevisiae*

Natural
PATTERN + PRINT

When creating a Natural Botanicals space, adding a few nature-inspired prints and patterns is key. Botanical motifs and designs can be found adorning many home accessories; for a natural look, hunt for designs with organic details that have been printed within the Natural Botanicals colour palette. I love the graceful, meticulously detailed botanical-inspired designs by Welsh designer and keen gardener Michael Angove – his designs can be found on his own wallpaper range and on products produced in collaboration with other homeware brands. I particularly like his dramatic black tray pattered with dill, ferns and an assortment of butterflies, which can be found at Hus & Hem.

Vintage prints and illustrations are one of the easiest ways to introduce some botanical styling into your home. Search vintage fairs and online sites such as Etsy and eBay for original or reproduction botanical illustrations. Once you have amassed a collection of

NATURAL DECORATING IDEAS

Single green stems in clear glass jars or vases make a lovely decoration when grouped on a mantelpiece or coffee table – I like to use grasses, ferns and feathery fennel. Dainty specimen vases, such as the ones above, showcase delicate fronds and flowers. Dried flowers, seed pods or berries add interest and texture, while houseplants are low maintenance and many of them clean the air in an interior. Use antique botanical prints to decorate walls – simply tape them up with masking tape or colourful washi tape, or find old wooden frames for a more permanent look. Ulster Weavers has used Royal Horticultural Society archive illustrations on a range of linen tea towels/dishtowels – a quick way to introduce botanical style into a kitchen. I love this passion flower design (above right).

prints, group them together on your wall or dot them around your space, propped up on mantelpieces or bookshelves, or pinned onto inspiration boards. I also like to hang prints using wooden trouser/pants hangers, which I buy online.

When choosing textiles, opt for natural linens and cotton with simple designs of delicate and trailing leaves. If pattern isn't your thing, use living or dried plants and flowers to add an additional layer of interest. Dried cotton bolls (*Gossypium hirsutum*, opposite above centre) add intriguing texture and colour, and of course houseplants, such as bromeliads (opposite above left), trailing mint (previous spread) and giant taro (*Alocasia macrorrhiza*, see page 130), offer a vast array of colours, tones and patterns.

BRING THE OUTDOORS IN

In this lofty London apartment, houseplants and potted herbs (above right) have been used to mirror the view through the picture windows. Larger-leafed plants, such as a castor oil plant (*Fatsia japonica*), occupy spacious corners (opposite), while smaller pots are clustered on tabletops and hanging plants at different heights add interest. The scale of the long branches cut from a kumquat tree (*Fortunella crassifolia*) and arranged in a giant glass jar is striking. If you have a view like this one, allow it to enjoy centre stage. Here, a deep pelmet covered in soft grey linen is all that is needed, as tall trees offer a sense of seclusion and privacy from the neighbours. Introducing different woods is another way to bring the outside in. Use untreated timber wherever possible (and practical) and mix up a variety for extra impact.

During the summer months when the trees outside are in full leaf, sitting at this table for a meal feels like dining in a treehouse (opposite). The old wooden table was found in a second-hand shop, while the black metal and wood chairs came from a French flea market. Wooden crates turned on one side (above left and right) make useful kitchen storage or an under-window display.

PLANT HARMONY

This multifunctional living space is divided into zones that are united by the houseplants, poppy seedheads and foliage. The low white display cabinet on the right separates the dining area from this end of the room, where a daybed loaded with cushions and throws provides a cosy spot for relaxation. The book cabinet and desk on the left are used as a home office.

ADD WARMTH WITH WOOD

The marble top of this antique chest of drawers
is home to a carefully curated display of natural finds,
ranging from a collection of shells to a glossy Swiss
cheese plant (*Monstera deliciosa*) sitting on a pile of
books (above). A hand-carved wooden dish holds a
collection of old scissors (above right). In this tranquil
bedroom, the bed frame and headboard are made
from rosewood and teamed with cotton bedding
and a vase of aromatic eucalyptus. When sourcing
wooden furniture or accessories, head to second-
hand shops or markets to find something unique.
Battered or chipped pieces do have charm, but always
check that they are repairable before handing over
your cash. A little light sanding or a re-stain are fairly
easy tasks, even if you're not a fan of DIY.

Make A BOTANICAL PINBOARD

Transform an old frame into a pretty pinboard to display an array of botanical postcards and prints. You will need a frame, spray paint, unsealed cork tiles, a craft knife, PVA glue and pins or tacks.

If your frame has glass in it, remove it and set aside the backboard. Wash the frame with warm, soapy water and let it dry. Take it outside and place it on newspaper, then use spray paint to cover the front of the frame (I used Matt Antique White from Plasti-Kote). Let it dry, then apply a second coat.

Next, place the cork tiles face down on a flat surface, put the backboard on top and mark around it with a pen. Use a craft knife to cut the cork to size. Glue the cork to the backboard with PVA glue and let it dry. Use the spray paint to give the cork a couple of coats of paint. Finally, slot the backboard into the frame and use pins or tacks to fix your botanical pictures in place.

Style Tip

Natural wood and lush greenery is a perfect combination when creating a botanical look. Accessorize a wooden desk or simple shelving with elements such as glass bottles, antique prints and, of course, a few houseplants. Here, old wooden crates stacked on the floor or hung on the wall provide interesting shelving as well as the perfect place to display pot plants, including a spider plant (*Chlorophytum comosum*) and a delta maidenhair fern (*Adiantum raddianum*). Look for wooden shelves and old crates at flea markets and junk stores. If you find a nice piece that's badly stained or coated in varnish, don't be put off – it won't take too much elbow grease to sand it back to its natural state.

Head outdoors in search of botanical additions for your home and take a few cuttings from shrubs and trees. In spring, collect branches laden with blossom; choose flowers and greenery in summer; colourful orange and red leaves in autumn; and berries and ivy in winter. An oak (*Quercus*) branch makes a striking display on this windowsill (right). On the sideboard and dining table (opposite and below), houseplants, including a mistletoe cactus (*Rhipsalis cassutha*), sit happily alongside foliage foraged from the garden, such as false Queen Anne's lace (*Ammi majus*), dill (*Anethum graveolens*) and berries.

FORAGED FROM THE GARDEN

Sourcing foliage from the garden is a budget-friendly way to introduce a botanical feel and a couple of leafy boughs make a big impact in any interior. Invest in a pair of secateurs, if you don't already own a pair, and some gardening gloves to protect your hands. If your garden isn't big enough to harvest a few stems or branches, or if you don't have any outdoor space, ask neighbours if there's anything they'd be happy for you to cut back, or look at what is growing wild near where you live. It is not usually an offence to cut foliage from a plant that's growing wild, as long as it's for your own personal use and you don't pull up or damage the roots in any way. Be warned that any plants growing in, for example, parks, roadsides or town or village displays are off limits, likewise those in nature reserves or community gardens.

NATURAL KITCHEN

The effect of the dark-stained wooden doors on these kitchen cupboards has been softened with the introduction of a couple of plants – an aloe in the foreground and a mistletoe cactus (*Rhipsalis cassutha*) on the far worktop – and masses of false Queen Anne's lace (*Ammi majus*) in a green cut-glass vase, along with some sprigs of dill (*Anethum graveolens*) and berry-laden branches, which add a pop of colour. To bring a natural feel to a kitchen, you need to introduce natural woods, and here a couple of worn chopping/cutting boards do the trick. A kitchen island is a good place to display plants in a kitchen – just make sure you leave enough room so that it still performs its function. Accessorize with a vintage enamel bread bin; this one has a few chips, but I think that adds to its charm. Terracotta plant pots also make great holders for utensils in natural kitchens.

HOUSEPLANT HEAVEN

Filling your home with houseplants can become a little addictive. They instantly transform a space, making it look fresher and more vibrant. With a huge variety of houseplants now available, there is something suitable for every space. Since working on this book, my living room has become a bit of a jungle and I've added an array of greenery to the mantelpiece (below left). This includes a couple of lacy delta maidenhair ferns (*Adiantum raddianum*), a lofty penstemon with coral pink flowers that I'll plant out in the garden come springtime and a faux tropical stem from Abigail Ahern. The plant on the floor to the left of the fireplace is a kentia palm (*Howea forsteriana*); these glossy beauties are easy to care for and will live happily in most positions as long as they are kept away from draughts.

Being surrounded by plants while you work is good for the soul and the air, and my home office is full of greenery (below). We painted this room white but left one wall bare, as we discovered beautiful plaster lurking beneath the previous wall covering. My creative space (opposite) has also been given the botanical treatment, with a selection of vintage prints on the wall and garden cuttings in glass jars.

This ingenious little homemade shelf was fashioned from a wooden offcut (below). A loop of sturdy string was slipped over either end and fixed to two screws in the wall. An extra piece of wood, again attached by string, was suspended beneath and acts as a place to dry out bunches of herbs, lavender and grasses. The dainty fern postcard is by the Swedish company Sköna Ting.

KEEP IT SIMPLE

I love the calming vibe in this simple yet elegant Swedish home, which belongs to a lovely florist and plant-shop owner. In one corner of the living room, a part-painted wall creates a defined gallery area where a collection of vintage mirrors hangs in harmony with vintage botanical prints and postcards (above). The worn leather armchair is a comfy place to curl up and relax. A novel idea for an interesting botanical-style vase is to hollow out the centre of a large tree branch or stump and fit a glass jar or plastic vase inside. Fill the concealed jar with water and greenery or flowers – here, white hydrangeas nestle among bamboo leaves. The dining space (opposite) boasts a mix of wooden chairs and is styled simply with a huge bottle vase displaying a curved branch cut from a tree in the garden. Placing houseplants along the windowsill allows them to enjoy adequate levels of daylight.

NATURAL STYLE

A classic palette of wood,
white, black and neutral
tones accented with plants
gives this living room a fresh,
natural feel. The windowsills
have been utilized to display
a mix of plants in baskets,
and illustrations of insects,
leaves and plants are stuck
to the walls with black tape.

PLANTS ON PARADE

For a quick but effective centrepiece with a Natural Botanicals theme, group single plant stems of varying heights in a collection of different vessels and vases (below). Here, I used an assortment of recycled glass jars and bottles, a dainty glass vase (a lucky junk-shop find) and a black ceramic vase. If you can't find a black vase, use spray paint to revamp one you already own. Antique glass vases and bottles can be sourced from markets and antiques shops – look for examples in pretty shades of green and check for cracks before buying. Glass bell jars or cloches look stylish and provide a microclimate for moisture-loving plants, as they maintain humidity levels and reduce the need for watering. Refresh the water in each vessel every couple of days so that it doesn't get stagnant – that way, your cuttings will stay fresh longer. A vintage wooden packing crate can be used as a display tray for an extra natural element.

Make A HAND-PRINTED CUSHION

For a 40 x 40cm/16 x 16in cushion pad/pillow form, you'll need a piece of unbleached cotton measuring 42 x 42cm/17 x 17in for the front and two pieces measuring 42 x 35cm/17 x 14in for the envelope back, a small paintbrush, black fabric paint, leaves, an iron and a sewing machine. Lay the pieces of fabric flat. Brush paint onto the veined backs of the leaves, then press them down firmly on the fabric. Continue printing in this way to create the desired effect. When the paint is dry, 'fix' it by pressing the fabric with a hot iron, as per the instructions. Sew a hem along the inner edge of each back section. Pin the front and back pieces with right sides together, overlapping the hems on the back pieces to make the central opening. Sew around all four sides, then turn the cover right side out and insert the pad.

In the eaves of this Swedish house, a snug bedroom with a white-painted wood-clad ceiling and natural wooden flooring is furnished in an eclectic style, with industrial drawers, a leather pouffe, a Moroccan wedding blanket and an Aztec-inspired rug. A couple of houseplants add a natural element, along with the pure linen and cotton bedding. I love the hippy dreamcatcher.

SOURCES

PLANTS & FLOWERS

Abigail Ahern
137 Upper Street
London N1 1QP
abigailahern.com
A gorgeous selection of faux plants, stems and flowers; visit the London store or shop online.

The Balcony Gardener
www.thebalconygardener.com
Gorgeous planted containers and terrariums. Garden design and lots of accessories and furniture for your garden and botanical home.

Columbia Road Flower Market
Columbia Road
London E2 7RG
www.columbiaroad.info
One of London's most visually appealing markets, it overflows with bucketfuls of beautiful flowers, every Sunday from 8am til 3pm come rain or shine.

David Austin Roses
Bowling Green Lane
Albrighton
Wolverhampton
WV7 3HB
01902 376334
www.davidaustinroses.com
Breeders of old English roses and specialist grower of the most fragrant roses. You can order bouquets of freshly cut blooms or plants to grown in your own garden. I collect different David Austin varieties in my own garden. It's also well worth visiting their fabulous rose garden in Shropshire.

The Fresh Flower Company
39a North Cross Road
East Dulwich
London SE22 9ET
www.freshflower.co.uk
A pretty flower shop supplying flowers for all occasions. They also have a workshop nearby where they host flower arranging classes and sell outdoor living products and a selection of houseplants.

The Joy of Plants
www.thejoyofplants.co.uk
A website full of plant tips and ideas for home décor – well worth a look if you're a plant lover!

Petersham Nurseries
Church Lane
off Petersham Road
Richmond
Surrey TW10 7AB
020 8940 5230
petershamnurseries.com
One of my favourite places to visit; an inspiring shop and nursery selling gorgeous botanical items for home and garden. There's also a tearoom and restaurant in a magical glasshouse setting.

Royal Horticultural Society
www.rhs.org.uk
Visit RHS gardens around the UK for inspiration as well as their flowers shows, including the prestigious Chelsea Flower Show; the most famous flower show in the UK, held every May since 1912.

Sarah Raven
www.sarahraven.com
A wide range of seeds, bulbs and plants plus floristry courses and gardening events.

Scarlet & Violet
79 Chamberlain Road
London NW10 3JJ
scarlet-violet.myshopify.com
Stunning, inspiring florist, well worth a visit. Amazing bouquets made from fresh flowers and a place full of botanical scents, chatter and creativity. I love it!

Terrain
www.shopterrain.com
Shop for inspiring home and garden decor, furniture, containers and seasonal plants. They have two stores in the USA, one in Westport and the other in Glen Mills. I'm dying to visit them both! In the meantime, I love following them on Pinterest @terrain

Wyevale Garden Centres
www.wyevalegardencentres.co.uk
151 stores across England and Wales offering a wide selection of plants for your garden and home.

Urban Jungle Bloggers
www.urbanjunglebloggers.com
For all green-loving friends, a place for bloggers to share ideas on how to create an urban jungle with DIYs and green tips – search their hashtag via social media: #urbanjunglebloggers

HOMEWARE & ACCESSORIES

Alfie's Studio
shop.alfies-studio.com
Lovely stationery and prints featuring hand-drawn botanical illustrations by Nicole.

An Angel at my Table
www.anangelatmytable.com
Online shop selling home accessories and furniture. I love their Boho & Co collection and their garden-room style items, including decorative urns, faux plants and 'Trees' fresco wallpaper.

Anthropologie
www.anthropologie.com
Unique ceramics and glassware with products sourced around the world. Stores across the USA and Europe, including a store in my home town of Guildford. A great source for boho style.

Avenida Isabel Ltd
www.avenidahome.com
Lovely tableware, linens, trays and ceramics. Look out for pieces designed by Michael Angove, Sarah Gillard and Nathalie Lété.

Cox & Cox
www.coxandcox.co.uk
Homeware, home accessories and gorgeous gifts.

Ercol
www.ercol.com
Quality handmade furniture company dating from 1920. Buy new items direct, or look out for vintage pieces of furniture at flea markets and antique shops.

Hagedornhagen
www.hagedornhagen.com
Botanical photography and art prints – I like their leaves, butterflies and beetles art prints.

Heart Vintage
www.heartvintage.co.uk
*Gorgeous floral designs
transferred to vintage plates and
ceramics, handmade botanical
stationery and home décor, all
handcrafted by independent
maker/designer Lisa Rushton.*

Homebarn
Wilton Farm
Marlow Road
Little Marlow
Buckinghamshire SL7 3RR
www.homebarnshop.co.uk
*A lovely shop in an old barn
selling an eclectic mix of industrial,
reclaimed, antique and retro.
I found a few gorgeous vintage
botanical prints, old glass lab
bottles and metal lockers.*

Hus & Hem
www.husandhem.co.uk
*Beautiful, functional and practical
Scandinavian homewares and
accessories that will brighten up
any home.*

IKEA
www.ikea.com
*Afforable modern furniture and
accessories for the home and
garden. Check out their selection
of houseplants and planters.*

Kith & Kin
kithandkin.org.uk
*Textile homewares designed by
Ciara Phelan – I love her leafy
tropical designs.*

Liberty
Regent Street
London W1B 5AH
www.liberty.co.uk

*One of London's oldest department
stores selling innovative and
eclectic designs with a wonderful
haberdashery department and
the glorious Nikki Tibbles Wild at
Heart fresh flower stall located
at the main entrance.*

Michael Angove
www.michaelangove.com
*Artist/designer and gardener
Michael's work is botanically
inspired. Shop his wallpaper designs
via Surface View and look out for
homeware collaborations with his
designs. I love his fennel and dill
design, which features on trays,
placemats and coasters.*

Paper Collective
www.paper-collective.com
*Iconic and unique design posters
and prints by top graphic designers,
artists and illustrators.*

Peony & Thistle
peonyandthistle.com
*A lovely independent maker and
vintage seller – check out the
homemade botanical bunting
and vintage botanical prints.*

Sköna Ting
www.skonating.com
*A Swedish company producing
prints, stationery, matchboxes and
decorative items with botanical
decorations.*

Smeg
www.smeg.com
*1950's style kitchen appliances –
a pastel green iconic fridge would
be the perfect addition to a
vintage/retro botanical kitchen.*

Sunbury Antiques Market
Kempton Park Racecourse
Staines Road East
Sunbury on Thames
Middlesex TW16 5AQ
www.sunburyantiques.com
*My nearest antiques market,
which is held the second and last
Tuesday of each month. A great
place to search out vintage, retro,
industrial and boho-style furniture.*

Surface View
www.surfaceview.co.uk
*Combines extraordinary imagery
with innovative technology to
create stunning bespoke prints,
wallpaper and handing murals.
They have a huge archive of
botanical images.*

Ulster Weavers
www.ulsterweavers.com
*Textile company that produces
botanical tea towels and floral
textile accessories.*

Wallography
www.wallography.co.uk
*Vintage Botanical wall charts
and posters and reproductions
from old science posters and
illustrations.*

WALLPAPER, PAINTS & FABRICS

Boråstapeter
www.borastapeter.se/en/
*Sweden's oldest wallpaper
company, with charming botanical
inspired designs. I love the 'Lilacs'
and 'Garden Party' patterns.*

Dulux
www.dulux.com
*A great selection of paints for
walls and wood and all botanical
themes, including black chalkboard
paint and moody colours perfect
for industrial botanical spaces.*

Ellie Cashman
www.elliecashmandesign.com
*Artist and designer Ellie Cashman
creates floral prints for wallpapers,
fabrics and accessories. Her iconic
dark floral designs are striking and
create an elegant botanical mood.*

Farrow & Ball
www.farrow-ball.com
*Great collection of paints and
wallpapers. I recommend their
Floor Primer and 'Great White'
Floor Paint for perfect Scandi-
inspired wooden floors.*

House of Hackney
131 Shoreditch High Street
London E1 6JE
www.houseofhackney.com
*Gorgeous luxurious, fashion-led
wallpapers, fabrics, home
accessories and clothing, all
sporting iconic designs, I love the
leafy 'Palmeral' wallpaper and
I have their 'Castanea' wallpaper,
inspired by British Chestnut trees,
in my bedroom. Their flagship
store is well worth a visit if you're
in London.*

Valspar
www.valsparpaint.com
*Fresh colours that are perfect
for botanical style interiors.
I especially love the fresh vintage
style of 'New Meadow' as well
as 'Spring Lawn' green.*

PICTURE CREDITS

All photography by Rachel Whiting, except where stated.

Endpapers Lindybug/istock; 1 The home and shop of Katarina von Wowern of www.minaideer.se; 2–3 The home of the author/stylist Selina Lake; 4 The London home of the interiors blogger Katy Orme (apartmentapothecary.com); 5 left The home and shop of Katarina von Wowern of www.minaideer.se; 5 right The home of Marie Emilsson www.trip2garden.se; 7–9 The home of the author/stylist Selina Lake; 10 Northwood Lodge, the home of interior designer and B&B owner Emma Clarke in Herne Bay, Kent/ph. Joanna Henderson; 11 left The home of the author/stylist Selina Lake; 11 right The South London home of Carole Poirot of www.mademoisellepoirot.com; 12 The home of the author/stylist Selina Lake; 13 Strömma Farm Lodge near Tvaaker in Sweden, Café and B&B www.strommafarmlodge.com; 14 The South London home of Carole Poirot of www.mademoisellepoirot.com; 15 left & right The garden of Viktoria Johansson of www.lillagrona.se; 15 centre and 16 left The home and shop of Katarina von Wowern of www.minaideer.se; 16 above right The Fresh Flower Company shop in East Dulwich; 16 below right The home of Marie Emilsson www.trip2garden.se; 17 The home and shop of Katarina von Wowern of www.minaideer.se; 18 above left ph. Georgia Glynn-Smith; 18 above right David Austin Roses. www.davidaustinroses.com/ph. Debi Treloar; 18 illustration by © Evgenii Naumov/Dreamstime.com; 18 below left ph. Debbie Patterson; 18 below right ph. Melanie Eclare; 19 above left SK Howard/istock;19 above centre ph. Pia Tryde; 19 above right Dentdelion/istock; 19 below left ph. Pia Tryde; 19 below centre W Wing/istock; 19 below right ph. Debbie Patterson; 20–21 The Fresh Flower Company shop in East Dulwich; 22 above The London home of the interiors blogger Katy Orme (apartmentapothecary.com); 22 below The garden of Viktoria Johansson of www.lillagrona.se; 24 left ph James Merrell; 24 right The home of the author/stylist Selina Lake; 25 left The home of Marie Emilsson www.trip2garden.se; 26–27 The home of the author/stylist Selina Lake; 28 The Fresh Flower Company workshop in East Dulwich; 30 The London home of the florist Fran Bailey of www.freshflower.co.uk; 31 Strömma Farm Lodge near Tvaaker in Sweden, Café and B&B www.strommafarmlodge.com; 32–33 The home of Marie Emilsson www.trip2garden.se; 34–35 Strömma Farm Lodge near Tvaaker in Sweden, Café and B&B www.strommafarmlodge.com; 35 illustration by godfather744431/istock; 38–39 background Strömma Farm Lodge near Tvaaker in Sweden, Café and B&B www.strommafarmlodge.com; 38 left and 39 left The London home of the interiors blogger Katy Orme (apartmentapothecary.com); 38 centre The London home of the florist Nikki Tibbles of Wild at Heart; 38 right The garden of Viktoria Johansson of www.lillagrona.se; 39 centre The home of the author/stylist Selina Lake; 40–42 Strömma Farm Lodge near Tvaaker in Sweden, Café and B&B www.strommafarmlodge.com; 43 below right–45 Strömma Farm Lodge near Tvaaker in Sweden, Café and B&B www.strommafarmlodge.com; 46–47 The home of the author/stylist Selina Lake; 48–49 Strömma Farm Lodge near Tvaaker in Sweden, Café and B&B www.strommafarmlodge.com; 50 illustration by © Evgenii Naumov/Dreamstime.com; 50 below left The London home of the interiors blogger Katy Orme (apartmentapothecary.com); 51 left The family home of Lea Bawnager, Vayu Robins and Elliot Bawnager-Robins, owner of affär/ph. Debi Treloar 51 right The family home of Shella Anderson, Tollesbury, UK/ph. Debi Treloar; 52–55 The London home of the interiors blogger Katy Orme (apartmentapothecary.com); 56–59 The garden of Viktoria Johansson of www.lillagrona.se; 58 illustration by © Evgenii Naumov/Dreamstime.com 60–61 Strömma Farm Lodge near Tvaaker in Sweden, Café and B&B www.strommafarmlodge.com; 61 illustration by Yantarj/Shutterstock.com; 64 left The home of Marie Emilsson www.trip2garden.se; 64 centre and right The London home of the florist Nikki Tibbles of Wild at Heart; 65 left The home of the author/stylist Selina Lake; 65 centre and right The London home of the florist Nikki Tibbles of Wild at Heart; 66–69 left Strömma Farm Lodge near Tvaaker in Sweden, Café and B&B www.strommafarmlodge.com; 69 right The home of the author/stylist Selina Lake; 69 illustration by © Evgenii Naumov/Dreamstime.com; 70–71 Strömma Farm Lodge near Tvaaker in Sweden, Café and B&B www.strommafarmlodge.com; 72–73 The home of the author/stylist Selina Lake; 73 illustration by © Evgenii Naumov/Dreamstime.com; 74 above Strömma Farm Lodge near Tvaaker in Sweden, Café and B&B www.strommafarmlodge.com; 74 below right and 75 The home of Marie Emilsson www.trip2garden.se; 76–81 The London home of the florist Nikki Tibbles of Wild at Heart; 82–83 The Fresh Flower Company workshop in East Dulwich; 83 background illustration by She/Shutterstock.com; 86 left The home and shop of Katarina von Wowern of www.minaideer.se; 86 right The Fresh Flower Company workshop in East Dulwich; 87 centre The home of Marie Emilsson www.trip2garden.se; 87 right–89 The home and shop of Katarina von Wowern of www.minaideer.se; 90–91 The home of Marie Emilsson www.trip2garden.se; 93 illustration by © Evgenii Naumov/Dreamstime.com; 94–95 The home of Marie Emilsson www.trip2garden.se; 96 The home and shop of Katarina von Wowern of www.minaideer.se; 97–101 The home of Marie Emilsson www.trip2garden.se; 108–109 right The home of the author/stylist Selina Lake; 109 left illustration by Ohmega1982/Shutterstock.com; 109 centre illustration by Pingwin/istock; 113 centre The Fresh Flower Company workshop in East Dulwich; 119 left The garden of Viktoria Johansson of www.lillagrona.se; 119 right The Fresh Flower Company workshop in East Dulwich; 119 illustration by © Evgenii Naumov/Dreamstime.com; 124 illustration by © Evgenii Naumov/Dreamstime.com; 130–131 The home and shop of Katarina von Wowern of www.minaideer.se; 131 left illustration by Lindybug/istock; 134 left The home of the author/stylist Selina Lake; 134 right The South London home of Carole Poirot of www.mademoisellepoirot.com; 134 right Northwood Lodge, the home of interior designer and B&B owner Emma Clarke in Herne Bay, Kent/ph. Joanna Henderson; 135 left The London home of the interiors blogger Katy Orme (apartmentapothecary.com); 135 centre The home and shop of Katarina von Wowern of www.minaideer.se; 135 right The London home of the interiors blogger Katy Orme (apartmentapothecary.com); 136–141 The South London home of Carole Poirot of www.mademoisellepoirot.com; 140 illustration by © Evgenii Naumov/Dreamstime.com; 142–143 left The London home of the florist Fran Bailey of www.freshflower.co.uk; 143 right The home and shop of Katarina von Wowern of www.minaideer.se; 144–145 The London home of the florist Fran Bailey of www.freshflower.co.uk; 146–147 The home of the author/stylist Selina Lake; 148–151 The home and shop of Katarina von Wowern of www.minaideer.se; 152 illustration by © Evgenii Naumov/Dreamstime.com; 152 right The home and shop of Katarina von Wowern of www.minaideer.se; 153 The home of Marie Emilsson www.trip2garden.se; 154–158 illustrations by © Evgenii Naumov/Dreamstime.com 157 The London home of the interiors blogger Katy Orme (apartmentapothecary.com); 160 Strömma Farm Lodge near Tvaaker in Sweden, Café and B&B www.strommafarmlodge.com.

BUSINESS CREDITS

Emma Clarke
Interior and garden design
E: Emma@eye-of-the-beholder.com
Pages 10, 134 right.

Marie Emilsson
Artist and florist
M: +46 738 067089
E: plan2trip@garden.se
www.trip2garden.se
Pages 5 right, 16 below right, 25 left, 32–33, 64 left, 74 below right, 75, 87 centre, 90–91, 94–95, 97–101, 153.

The Fresh Flower Company Ltd
39 Northcross Road
London SE22 9ET
T: 020 8693 6088
www.freshflower.co.uk
Pages 16 above right, 20–21, 28, 30, 82–83, 86 right, 113 centre, 119 right, 142–143 left, 144–145.

Viktoria Johansson
Garden designer
M: +46 (0)702 485261
E: victoria@lillagrona.se
www.lillagrona.se
Pages 15 left, 15 right, 22 below, 38 right, 56–59, 119 left.

Selina Lake
Author & stylist
www.selinalake.co.uk
www.selinalake.blogspot.co.uk
Instagram and Pinterest:
@selinalake
Pages 2–3, 7–9, 11 left, 12, 24 right, 26–27, 39 centre, 46–47, 65 left, 69 right, 72–73, 108–109 right, 134 left, 146–147.

Katy Orme
Interiors blogger and stylist
www.apartmentapothecary.com
Pages 4, 22 above, 38 left, 39 left, 50 below, 52–55, 135 left and right, 157.

Carole Poirot
Stylist and photographer
www.mademoisellepoirot.com
Pages 11 right, 14, 134 right, 136–141.

Strömma Farm Lodge
Café and B&B
Strömma 6
432 77 Tvååker
Sweden
E: info@strommafarmlodge.com
www.strommafarmlodge.com
Pages 13, 31, 34–35, 38–30 background, 40–42, 43 below right, 44–45, 48–49, 60–61, 66–69 left, 70–71, 74 above, 160.

Katarina von Wowern
Florist and visual merchandiser
www.minaideer.se
Pages 1, 5 left, 15 centre, 16 left, 17, 86 left, 87 right, 88, 89, 96, 130, 131, 135 centre, 143 right, 148–151, 152 right.

Nikki Tibbles Wild at Heart
Florist
222 Westbourne Grove
London W11 2RH
T: +44(0) 20 7727 3095
E: island@wildatheart.com
wildatheart.com
Nikki Tibbles' own home, interior designed with Carden Cunietti:
Pages 38 centre, 64 centre, 64 right, 65 centre, 65 right, 76–81.

For more inspiration, check out my favourite
Botanical Instagrammers:

@seedtostem
@ivymuse_melb
@willowcrossleyflowers
@sproutlondon
@shopterrain
@urbanjungleblogger
@trip2garden
@hakesgard

@lillagrona_viktoria
@quincebrighton
@theborrowednursery
@zetastradgard
@botanyshope5
@arstidensbasta
@minaideer
@gandgorgeousflowers

INDEX

Page numbers in *italic* refer
to the illustrations

Acknowledgments

Firstly, a big thank you to my publishers Ryland Peters & Small and everyone who worked on this project with me. I can't believe this is my seventh book!

Huge thanks to Rachel Whiting for your lovely photography. I really enjoyed working with you – especially on our mini break in rainy Sweden, where we discovered chocolate *Delicatobolls*, sheltered from the rain in a pretty greenhouse and got to know the beautiful Swedish countryside.

I so enjoyed visiting all the wonderful botanical locations while shooting this book – the amazing plant shops, florists, warehouses, gardens, guest houses, wedding venues, interior shops, barns and unique homes. Big thanks to all the lovely owners who made Rachel and me feel welcome. Thanks also for the snacks and cups of tea, which kept us going on the long days.

Thank you to all the companies, independent makers and designers who loaned me items and products to use while I was styling this book. Check out the Sources and Business Credits on pages 154–157.

To all my social-media followers, thanks for your tweets, comments and blog posts. If you've been inspired by any of the styling ideas or makes in *Botanical Style*, I'd love to see your pictures. Find me @selinalake on Pinterest, Instagram, Twitter and Facebook. #BotanicalStyle

Last but not least, thank you to my wonderful family: my parents Valerie and Ronald, who always support me, buy plants for our garden and have helped me grow; my grandmothers, Doreen Howard-Baylis, who loved fuchsias and giving my mum cuttings from her plants, and Lilian Lake, who enjoyed painting flowers (I used some of her paintings in 'Boho Botanicals'). Finally, a big thank you to my husband, who does all the hard graft in our garden – laying paths, maintaining the lawn, fixing our shed and making raised beds – as well as all the DIY indoors. Thanks for making our house a home and for enjoying a visit to a garden centre as much as I do! Love you x